"At first I thought this would be gross, but it was really tasty. It is great for a party because you can set it up buffet style and people can take what they like. I really don't eat much red meat anymore, so I would be so happy to have these instead of beef tacos."

DANIELLE

"It's so much more satisfying to eat it and know you made it."

ROSIE

"This is a more natural way to make the dressing than using store-bought mayo, and you don't risk the salmonella. Everyone loved the dressing. When you hear 'fish sauce,' you might go 'yuck,' but it really gave it a yummy flavor."

DANIELLE

SAY: HEE-KAH-MAH

A CINCH TO PREPARE

YUMMY

"The best times are when my friends get together, play our favorite music really loud, and cook some of our favorite food."

IAN

GET COOKING!

"It is amazing how easy and fun it can be to cook foods I thought I would only be able to order in restaurants. Following these recipes made it easy. It is fun to see how a table full of ingredients can be transformed into meals that we prepared."

IAN

"Rozanne's recipes rock!"

STEPH & ROSIE

"I made up this recipe using granola because I really like snacking on it. It is very natural, but also sweet and crunchy. I thought it would make a nice topping for the soft cooked apples. After apple picking in the fall, when you have a nice mixture of fresh apples, this is a fun recipe to make."

DANIELLE

FUN TO EAT

"I love to chop and prepare vegetables with my sharp knives."

DAN

ZINGY!

"I really like using my hands to mix a bowl full of food. It feels like you really get to know the ingredients when you touch them."

ROBYN

ADDICTIVE!

"I never thought of myself as a great cook, but following these recipes turned me into one."

IAN

"I love cooking in my kitchen. When I'm alone in there, I can really think about flavors and create wonderful foods, but I also like when my friends and I get together to cook. It always feels like a party."

ROBYN

SPICY!

LOGAN SQUARE BRANCH

EAT
FRESH FOOD

AWESOME RECIPES
FOR TEEN CHEFS

Published by Bloomsbury U.S.A. Children's Books
175 Fifth Avenue, New York, New York 10010

Library of Congress Cataloging-in-Publication Data
Gold, Rozanne.
Eat fresh food / by Rozanne Gold and her all-star team ;
photographs by Phil Mansfield. — 1st U.S. ed.
p.   cm.
"Awesome recipes for teen chefs."
ISBN-13: 978-1-59990-282-1 • ISBN-10: 1-59990-282-6 (hardcover)
ISBN-13: 978-1-59990-445-0 • ISBN-10: 1-59990-445-4 (paperback)
1. Cookery—Juvenile literature. I. Mansfield, Phil. II. Title.
TX652.5.G5457 2009   641.5—dc22   2008042443

Book design by Matthew Bouloutian and Vivian Ghazarian

First U.S. Edition 2009
Printed in Singapore by Tien Wah Press
(hardcover) 10 9 8 7 6 5 4 3 2 1
(paperback) 10 9 8 7 6 5 4 3 2 1

All papers used by Bloomsbury U. S. A. are natural, recyclable
products made from wood grown in well-managed forests.
The manufacturing processes conform to the environmental
regulations of the country of origin.

NOTE ABOUT THIS BOOK:

As with almost any cookbook, this one includes recipes that require cooking with heat and cutting with sharp implements, including knives and graters. Any child in a kitchen should be supervised by a parent or guardian. The creators of this cookbook take no responsibility for unsupervised cooking by a child—but have included guidelines for safer cooking.

EAT
~~FRESH~~ FOOD

AWESOME RECIPES
FOR TEEN CHEFS

Rozanne Gold AND ▷ HER ALL-STAR TEAM
MORE THAN 80 RECIPES!
PHOTOGRAPHS BY ▷ PHIL MANSFIELD

COOK THIS BOOK!

BLOOMSBURY

NEW YORK BERLIN LONDON

This book is dedicated
to my beautiful family:
Michael, Jeremy, Shayna, and
to the memory of my mother
and father, Marion Gold
and Bill Gold
—R. G.

For K, C,
and B
—*P. M.*

INTRODUCTION
page ⇨ 8

 BREAD, BUTTER & BREAKFAST
page ⇨ 17

BOWLS: SOUPS & PASTA
page ⇨ 35

SANDWICHES, BURGERS & PIZZA
page ⇨ 55

SALADS, BIG & SMALL
page ⇨ 71

DINNER SPECIALS WITH VEGETABLES
page ⇨ 91

 SIDE DISHES
page ⇨ 107

DESSERTS & DRINKS
page ⇨ 121

MENUS
page ⇨ 152

ACKNOWLEDGMENTS
page ⇨ 156

INDEX
page ⇨ 157

There is a noisy **REVOLUTION** afoot led by a brigade of aspiring **YOUNG CHEFS** who are clamoring for time in the kitchen, who have added "cooking" and "eating responsibly" to their list of favorite activities. **EAT FRESH FOOD** is a guide to experiencing the joys of cooking—including **EXCURSIONS** to farmers' markets, shopping for super-fresh ingredients, and sharing the edible **REWARDS** with family and friends. It comes with excellent advice for healthy eating on every page. The cookbook focuses on **FRESH**, natural, and unprocessed food, with vegetables or fruits being the stars of each dish. The recipes and **TECHNIQUES** are from a professional chef supported by the skills, inspirations, and **TASTE BUDS** of a team of **HAPPY SOUS-CHEFS** ranging in age from nine to nineteen. It is their book as much as it is mine.

Every recipe was tested and tasted by my team: executive sous-chef Evan Chender, age 19, who provided the inspiration for the book; sous-chefs extraordinaire Danielle Hartog, age 14; Shayna DePersia, age 13; Ian Kimmel, age 16; Robyn Kimmel, age 9; and a brigade of friends—some older, some younger—many of whom helped with the creation of my previous book *Kids Cook 1-2-3*.

All of the food is healthful. With the guidance of nutritionist Helen Kimmel, who has worked with me on all of my books, the goal was to create recipes that were delicious and *real* (see Helen's notes on page 11). The criteria for inclusion were that "the team" loved the recipes, had a good time making them, and learned about ingredients. They baked bread from scratch, whipped cream into butter, made marmalade from carrots instead of oranges, fashioned summer cherries into bright red ices, roasted vegetables, and cooked proteins in ways that demonstrated their unique characteristics.

For better nutrition and more vibrant flavor, we substituted fresh vegetable purees for cream and butter in several recipes. A coral-colored puree of red bell peppers provides the background for a rich-tasting cheddar cheese sauce for macaroni; zucchini gets whirled into a gorgeous jade sauce for pasta primavera; cauliflower, not potatoes, gets star billing in a delicious side dish called Looks Like Mashed Potatoes; and olive oil is the fat of choice in most of the cakes and muffins.

I believe that butter, sugar (especially raw, or turbinado, sugar), honey, real maple syrup, unbleached organic white and whole-wheat flour, cheese, red meat, and chocolate can be enjoyed in responsible ways, especially if they play supporting roles. In this book, they do.

As we tested these recipes, I was surprised but delighted to learn that the tasters really enjoyed the healthier dishes and that one of the team's favorite recipes turned out to be . . . Very Fresh Vegetable Soup (which you will find on page 38) made from eight farmers'-market vegetables. It doesn't get real-er or fresher than that!

My brigade of young chefs produced food that truly is beautiful. Nature provides us with a rainbow of colors, and all good chefs know that we feast with our eyes first before we pop any morsel into our mouths. Our job is to simply maximize the inherent qualities of what grows every season.

We agree wholeheartedly with Michael Pollan, who, in his excellent book *In Defense of Food,* urges us to "eat food; not too much; mostly plants." We add to that:

MAKE IT FRESH!

HERE'S HOW:

F= Farmer-friendly

Take a large map of the area you live in and, using your house as the center, draw a circle with a diameter of 100 miles. Using the Internet, find as many local farmers as you can within that circle and go visit! A person who eats food that is produced close to home is called a "locavore."

R= Ripe-ready

The best recipes use the best ingredients, and the best ingredients are those that are ripe and ready to eat. *Do* judge a vegetable by its color. In order to determine whether something is ripe (or overripe), you must *smell* it. Put it right under your nose and take a big whiff. Yes, you will experience the essence of the fruit or vegetable or cheese by smelling it; 70 percent of taste is smell.

E= Easy-exciting

These recipes are surprisingly easy to make with exciting new techniques and tastes for you to discover. Throughout the book you will read some of my sous-chefs' comments about the process and how gratifying it was to cook food that was easy to make, beautiful to look at, and delicious to eat.

S= Sustainable

Sustainable foods are those that don't harm the environment. You are making sustainable food choices when you choose foods that are in season, are grown locally, and, when available, are grown without chemicals. Look for ingredients that say "natural," "vine-ripened," "free-range," or "organic."

H= Honest-healthy

Honest meals are those that are fresh and real and are put together in ways that respect the inherent goodness of their ingredients. With all fresh, unprocessed food comes a wealth of beneficial vitamins and nutrients, *none* of which we should miss. Nutritionists wisely advise us to eat all the colors and to eat a large variety of foods. This book offers more than eighty ways to do it!

NOTES FROM OUR NUTRITIONIST

While teens have made multitasking the norm—texting, IMing, and surfing Web pages *while* doing their homework—they have also been bombarded with media messages for processed food products and energy drinks crammed with artificial ingredients and colors in trendy packages that are supposed to fit into their hectic lives, and into the lives of their harried parents. This has led to disastrous levels of obesity and childhood diabetes, to sedentary lifestyles, and to the dissolution of family meals.

The message is simply... eat fresh food. And Rozanne shows you how to make cooking an integral part of your day. By allowing yourselves to take a little time to prepare these recipes, you'll see that the kitchen is both a place to gather your friends *and* a place to enjoy some time alone. Along the way you will learn the true pleasure of cooking with real ingredients, and soon you won't need, or desire, chemical-laden, overprocessed food as part of your diet. The bonus is that when you eat fresh food, you may not crave the quick pick-me-ups of hypercaffeinated, supersugared drinks and supersized portions.

Instead of bombarding you with lots of nutritional numbers, we have done the work for you by creating recipes that are based on fresh, unprocessed ingredients; balanced; trans fat–free; and as low as possible in saturated fat.

The "rules" about saturated fats have changed over the years, but it has always been believed that mono- and polyunsaturated fats are good. We've kept the bad saturated fats as low as we can, without worrying about the good fats (such as olive oil) and without sacrificing taste. We realize that if it doesn't taste good, you won't eat it, no matter how healthy it is. We've made our portions (and the calories in these portions)

"A little fresh basil, tomato, mozzarella, and I am in heaven."
KILLIAN

a realistic size. I laugh when my young daughter can eat what is supposed to be four servings of something because the serving size is so small. We know you are active and growing and need lots of good food to keep going.
—Helen Kimmel, M.S., R.D.

ABOUT ORGANIC FOOD

Organic fruits and vegetables are grown in clean soil without the use of chemical pesticides or chemical fertilizers. Because of this, the fruits and vegetables are also free from these chemicals. Organic foods used to be produced only by small farms. Within the last few years, larger farms and companies have begun to grow and produce organic foods, so now they are more widely available. Organic farming is better for the environment, producing less pollution that can harm soil, water, and wildlife.

However, it is nearly impossible (and very expensive) to eat only organics. Certain foods absorb more chemicals than others. As a general rule, fruits and vegetables with a thick skin that is peeled and discarded (such as oranges, bananas, and onions) contain fewer chemicals than foods with edible skin (such as peaches, apples, and berries). If organic edible-skin items are available, consider buying them.

When buying fish, try to find wild varieties. Farm-raised (or "ocean-raised") fish live cramped together in very small farm ponds. Because of this, they don't get to swim and develop properly, have an increased rate of disease, and are fed manufactured foods and antibiotics. Wild fish have been shown to be healthier and to taste better.

When buying poultry, meat, and eggs, choose products that are labeled "free range" and/or "organic" and come from a specific farm or are part of a special breed. "Free-range" means that the animals are treated more humanely, with a bit more room to exercise and develop. Non-labeled (regular) meats are from animals that are crowded together and may be fed foods laced with hormones and drugs. "Certified organic" means that the animals were fed a natural diet and were not exposed to chemicals or pesticides. Organic milk comes from cows that have had no hormones or antibiotics, so the milk is also free of these substances.

"I like to think of new ways to use the flavors and ingredients I like best. I love to go to the farmers' market and buy some fruit and vegetables that are new to me, then go home and taste each one."

ROBYN

THE PANTRY

Of course, there's more to good cooking than what comes directly from the farm, and here you will find a list of pantry staples that every good cook should have on hand. These are the spices, vinegars, oils, global condiments, and necessities—such as canned tomatoes and chickpeas—that you would find in a professional chef's pantry.

Keep in mind that **salt** (I use kosher salt), **black peppercorns** (always freshly ground from a pepper mill), and **fresh water** should be on hand at all times. They are the fundamentals of cooking and so they are not listed in the ingredient list of each recipe. Instead, they appear in the procedures, where sometimes specific amounts are called for and in other cases instructions are given for adding salt and pepper "to taste." Just like the professional chefs do.

Kosher salt

Whole black peppercorns

Baking powder

Baking soda

Whole-wheat flour

Self-rising flour

Unbleached white flour

Real maple syrup

Honey

Pure almond extract

Pure vanilla extract

Vanilla beans

Granulated sugar

Ground cinnamon

Cinnamon sticks

Sesame seeds

Dried oregano leaves

Ground cumin

Chili powder

Curry powder

Red pepper flakes

Ground allspice

Turbinado sugar

Dark brown sugar

Tabasco or sriracha sauce

Tamari

Asian sesame oil

Olive oil

Vegetable oil

Rice vinegar

Balsamic vinegar

Unsulfured molasses

Apple cider vinegar

Hoisin/barbecue sauce

Thai fish sauce

Light coconut milk

Steel-cut oats

Dijon mustard

Ketchup

Tomato juice

Whole tomatoes in puree

Organic chicken broth

Dried pasta: various shapes

Bulgur wheat

Canned chickpeas

Sun-dried tomatoes in oil

Pecans, walnuts, pine nuts

Raisins

EQUIPMENT

You don't need lots of fancy equipment to make great food. I use only a few **pots** and **pans** and I have a collapsible **metal steamer basket** that can be inserted into a medium pot for quickly steaming vegetables. I have a **wok** and several very large **nonstick skillets** with covers. You will need a **food processor** and a free-standing **electric mixer** or a **handheld mixer**. A **box grater** is essential, and I love using a **Microplane** for zesting lemons, limes, and oranges. A simple, inexpensive **ice cream maker** will come in handy for the frozen treats. A variety of **saucepans** is necessary: small (2-quart), medium (4-quart), and large (6- to 8-quart). A very **large pot** for boiling pasta is also important to have. A **food mill** is a good idea for making fresh tomato sauce.

You do NOT need a microwave (I don't own one). You DO need a set of heavy sharp **knives**, including a paring knife (with a blade that is 3 to 4 inches long), a 6-inch utility knife, a 9-inch chef's knife, and a serrated knife (with a jagged blade) for slicing bread, tomatoes, and citrus fruit.

Other small wares include **measuring spoons and cups**, a sharp **vegetable peeler, cutting boards**, rimmed **baking sheets**, a **garlic press, mixing bowls, parchment paper**, a **potato masher, wooden spoons, wire whisks, flexible rubber spatulas**, a **wire mesh strainer, pastry brushes**, and a **colander**. A **kitchen scale** is an indispensable tool for consistent results.

And a **Silpat pad** is nice for baking cookies.

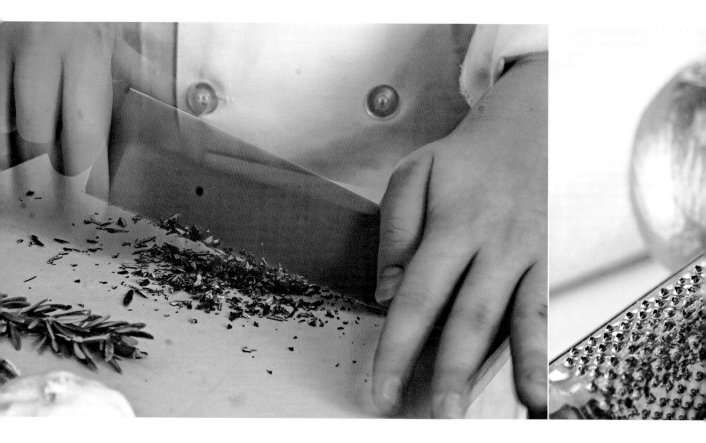

SAFETY

Be aware of safety when using any kind of equipment. Wear sturdy shoes just in case anything falls near your feet. Don't wear loose clothing or wide sleeves. If you have long hair, pull it back or wear a chef's hat. Always use potholders, and don't let pot handles stick out over the front of the stove.

Use the right knife for the right job, keep it sharp, and always use a cutting board. To keep it firmly in place, put a damp kitchen towel underneath.

Always turn the oven or stovetop to the "off" position as soon as you finish with it. Be careful to leave a small opening at the top of the food processor when pureeing hot liquids in order to let the steam escape.

Go slowly and concentrate on every step.

GETTING STARTED

Wash your hands thoroughly with soap and water. Roll up your sleeves, or put on a chef's jacket just like the sous-chefs who worked on this project did. Wearing whites can inspire you to work like a pro. It is important to read a recipe carefully before you start cooking. This way you will know what ingredients you need to buy and what utensils you will need. You will also determine (depending on your size, age, and experience) whether you need a **kitchen buddy** to help you with some of the more difficult techniques or even just the heavy lifting!

It's a good idea to set all your ingredients out in front of you at the start of the recipe. This is known as *mise en place*, or everything in its place. Measure the ingredients and prepare them carefully according to the instructions in each recipe. Now you are ready to *COOK THIS BOOK!*

a loaf of whole-wheat bread ⇨ 19

homemade butter ⇨ 21

sweet carrot jam ⇨ 21

tender muffins: country pear, cinnamon-apple, or blueberry ⇨ 22

"tunkalee" with farm-fresh scrambled eggs ⇨ 23

awesome oats with green apples, dried cherries, and sunflower seeds ⇨ 24

ultra-thin breakfast crepes with fresh blueberry syrup ⇨ 26

grape-and-pignoli breakfast cake ⇨ 28

"pink flamingo" yogurt smoothie ⇨ 30
SIDEBAR: HOW TO DEAL WITH A MANGO 30

pineapple-coconut frullato ⇨ 33

A LOAF OF WHOLE-WHEAT BREAD

Put aside approximately three and a half hours for baking this delicious bread. This includes the time for two risings, baking, and cooling. Granulated yeast can be found in any supermarket, right next to the flour. "Kneading" the dough means that you press it down hard, fold it over itself, then press again. You do it at least twenty-five times per rising. Lightly flour your hands, not the counter, as you go along. In this recipe, the surprise addition of cocoa powder adds a hint of flavor and turns the bread a lovely color. ➡ **MAKES 1 LOAF (14 TO 16 SLICES)**

1 package granulated yeast

1 tablespoon sugar

1½ cups whole-wheat flour

½ cup all-purpose unbleached white flour, plus more for your hands

1 tablespoon unsweetened cocoa powder

½ cup milk, at room temperature

2 teaspoons olive oil, for greasing the loaf pan

❶ Put ½ cup of warm tap water in a small bowl. Stir in the yeast and sugar until dissolved. Let sit for 10 minutes or until it bubbles and doubles in volume.

❷ Put both flours, cocoa, and ½ teaspoon salt in the bowl of a standing mixer (or in a large bowl that can be used with electric beaters). Mix briefly. Add the dissolved yeast and mix until crumbly. Add the milk and beat until the dough forms a ball that pulls away from the sides of the bowl. The dough will be the tiniest bit sticky. Roll onto a clean counter and knead 25 times (lightly flouring your hands as needed). Roll into a smooth ball. Put into a large clean bowl and pull plastic wrap tightly over the top. You can do your homework or watch it rise! Let rise for 1½ hours, or until the dough has doubled in volume and is a little spongy.

❸ Punch the dough down again and knead on the counter about 25 times. Lightly oil a loaf pan (8½ x 4½ inches or a 6-cup pan of any shape) and pat the dough into the pan, making sure to press it down into the corners. Cover with a kitchen towel and let it rise for 1 hour, until the dough has risen by half.

❹ During the second rising, heat the oven to 400 degrees. Bake the bread for 35 minutes, until firm to the touch. Let cool for 10 minutes, then turn it out of the pan. Cool before slicing.

TASTY

"I never thought it possible that kids like us could make food like this!"

STEPH

HOMEMADE BUTTER

It is so easy, and lots of fun, to make butter at home. All you need is heavy cream and salt . . . and a sturdy electric mixer. You beat it and beat it and after a while the solids separate from the whey (the milky liquid), leaving you with a ball of pale butter. The flavor develops as it sits.

▷ **MAKES ABOUT ½ CUP**

1 cup heavy cream

Large pinch of salt

❶ Put the cream in the bowl of an electric mixer. Let sit for 15 minutes to warm up. Use a bowl guard or wrap the bowl and top of the mixer over the arm in plastic wrap (to prevent the cream from splattering everywhere). Beat on high speed for 7 minutes. The cream will begin to thicken and become smooth. Then it will change suddenly and separate into small solids and a milky liquid. A few seconds later, a ball of butter will form.

❷ Drain off the liquid and press down on the butter to release all the liquid. Mush it around with a large spoon to "knead" it. Add a large pinch of salt to taste and stir well. Put the butter in a ramekin or a small cup. You can spread it on bread right now or cover and refrigerate it for up to 1 week.

SWEET CARROT JAM

This is a very popular jam in Egypt. It looks a lot like orange marmalade and lasts a long time in the fridge. Yum.

▷ **MAKES ABOUT 2 CUPS**

1 pound carrots

2 cups sugar

3 tablespoons freshly squeezed lemon juice

❶ Peel the carrots, cut them into 1½-inch pieces, and put in the bowl of a food processor. Pulse until they are coarsely ground (about ⅛-inch pieces). You will have about 3 cups. Put the carrots in a heavy 4-quart medium-size pot. Add the sugar, lemon juice, 1 cup water, and a pinch of salt. Bring to a rapid boil and cook for 1 minute. Lower the heat to medium and cook for about 1 hour, stirring frequently.

❷ To see if it is ready to jell, place 1 tablespoon of the mixture on a small plate and put in the freezer for 1 minute. If it becomes firm and doesn't flow, it is done even though it will still look quite liquid in the pot. Remove the pot from the heat and let cool. Spoon the mixture into a jar. Cover and refrigerate.

A SPECIAL TREAT

Stir lots of carrot jam into plain yogurt and top with crushed pistachios. Good for breakfast, as a snack, or for dessert.

TENDER MUFFINS: COUNTRY PEAR, CINNAMON-APPLE, OR BLUEBERRY

These muffins are moist and delicate and can be made with ripe pears, tart apples, or fresh blueberries. They are a cinch to prepare and last several days in a tightly covered tin. ⇨ **MAKES 9 MUFFINS**

1½ cups self-rising flour

¾ cup granulated sugar

1 teaspoon ground cinnamon
   (or 1½ teaspoons if using apples)

1 extra-large egg

½ cup buttermilk

⅓ cup olive oil

1¼ cups diced peeled apples, or peeled
   ripe pears, or fresh blueberries

2 tablespoons turbinado sugar

❶ Preheat the oven to 350 degrees. Line 9 muffin tins with paper liners.
❷ Stir together the flour, granulated sugar, and cinnamon in a large bowl. In a medium bowl, beat together the egg, buttermilk, and olive oil. Pour the wet mixture into the dry mixture and stir with a flexible rubber spatula until a batter forms. Gently stir in the fruit.
❸ Scoop the batter into the muffin tins. Sprinkle with the turbinado sugar. Bake for 25 minutes or until golden and firm to the touch. Let cool.

A CINCH TO PREPARE

22

"TUNKALEE" WITH FARM-FRESH SCRAMBLED EGGS

I ate this colorful dish growing up, and I love it still. Its funny name comes from my mother, who said it sounded like something she heard growing up in her Hungarian-speaking home. Perfect for breakfast or lunch, this simple egg dish is based on *lesco*, a combination of sautéed onions, green bell peppers, and tomatoes that appears in many Hungarian recipes. ⇨ **SERVES 4**

1 tablespoon unsalted butter

1½ tablespoons olive oil

1 large onion, cut into ¼-inch cubes

1 medium green bell pepper, cut into ¼-inch cubes

1 medium yellow or orange bell pepper, cut into ¼-inch cubes

3 large ripe tomatoes

7 extra-large eggs plus 3 egg whites

❶ Melt the butter and oil in a very large nonstick skillet over very low heat. Add the onions and cook until soft, about 5 minutes, stirring often. Add the bell peppers and cook over medium heat for 10 minutes, stirring often.

❷ Cut the tomatoes in half and squeeze out the seeds. Cut the tomatoes into small pieces, add to the pan, and stir. Add salt and pepper to taste. Cook 10 minutes or until soft.

❸ Beat the eggs, egg whites, and a large pinch of salt. Stir the beaten eggs into the vegetables, and scramble over medium-high heat with a flexible rubber spatula. Cook and stir until the eggs are softly scrambled and just set.

AWESOME OATS WITH GREEN APPLES, DRIED CHERRIES, AND SUNFLOWER SEEDS

Steel-cut oats are a bit chewier than "rolled" oats, and that's why we love them. Adding lots of grated apple makes them especially juicy. Try substituting raisins or dried cranberries for the cherries. ▷ **SERVES 4**

3 tablespoons dark brown sugar

1 cup steel-cut oats

1 large Golden Delicious apple

½ cup dried cherries

¼ cup sunflower seeds

❶ Bring 4 cups of water to a boil in a medium-size saucepan. Add 1 tablespoon of the brown sugar and a large pinch of salt; stir a little bit to dissolve. Pour in the oats and stir over high heat for about 5 minutes. Reduce the heat and simmer, uncovered, for 20 minutes, stirring often.

❷ Wash the apple and dry well. Do not peel. Cut it in half, lengthwise, and discard the seeds. Grate each half on the large holes of a box grater, starting with the cut side.

❸ After 20 minutes, add the grated apples (and any juice) and the dried cherries to the oatmeal. Cook over low heat for 5 to 10 minutes, stirring frequently, until the oatmeal is thick and creamy. Transfer to bowls and garnish with the sunflower seeds or apple slices. Crumble the remaining brown sugar on top.

"Some people
like to draw or paint,
but for me, cooking is one
of the ways I love to express myself.
I like to show people I care
about them by cooking their favorite
foods and watching
their faces when they eat."

· · · · · · · · · ·
ROBYN

ULTRA-THIN BREAKFAST CREPES WITH FRESH BLUEBERRY SYRUP

When the movie *Ratatouille* came out, our friends Robyn and Ian Kimmel made these crepes on camera for a promotional DVD, produced by the Food Network's Marc Summers. Robyn and Ian created this recipe and topped it with freshly made blueberry syrup. Use thick Greek yogurt to dollop on crepes. ▷ **SERVES 6**

"Seeing how easy it is to make something fancy like crepes made me realize that I can cook anything I want."

IAN

fresh blueberry syrup

2½ cups fresh blueberries

2 tablespoons honey

**2 teaspoons freshly squeezed
    lemon juice**

crepes

2 extra-large eggs

1 cup unbleached white flour

1¼ cups milk

2 tablespoons unsalted butter, melted

¾ cup plain Greek yogurt

A handful of fresh raspberries

❶ To make the blueberry syrup: Put 1½ cups of the blueberries and the honey in a heavy saucepan. Cook over medium heat and stir often until they burst, about 6 minutes. Add the remaining blueberries and cook until slightly thickened, about 3 minutes. Add lemon juice. Remove from heat.

❷ To make the crepes: Preheat the oven to 250 degrees. Break the eggs into a large bowl, add ¼ teaspoon salt, and whisk well. Add several spoonfuls of the flour and whisk (at this point, it will be a bit lumpy, but that is okay). Whisk one third of the milk into the batter. Alternate adding some flour and then some milk, whisking until smooth after each addition. Stir in the melted butter.

❸ To cook the crepes: Preheat an 8-inch nonstick skillet over medium heat. Add ¼ cup of the batter to the center of the pan. As you pour in the batter with one hand, use the other to twirl the pan around to coat the bottom with the batter. If there are empty spots, add some extra batter. After about a minute, the edges of the crepe will become lacy looking, but the top will still look moist. Slip a plastic spatula under the crepe and flip it over. When the second side has cooked for about 20 seconds, slip the crepe out of the pan and onto a plate. Continue to make 12 crepes (total), keeping them on an ovenproof platter in the oven, covered loosely with foil.

❹ Fold each crepe in quarters and top with gently warmed blueberry syrup and a dollop of yogurt. Scatter with a few fresh raspberries.

GRAPE-AND-PIGNOLI BREAKFAST CAKE

Not too sweet, but full of flavor, this moist breakfast cake is an original spin on more ordinary coffee cakes. My daughter, Shayna, is a grape freak and thinks the cake is "divine." It lasts several days in a tightly covered tin. ⇨ **SERVES 10**

12 ounces red seedless grapes

2 extra-large eggs

¼ cup milk

½ cup plus one tablespoon olive oil

1 teaspoon vanilla extract

Grated zest of 1 lemon

½ cup plus 1 tablespoon sugar

1½ cups self-rising flour

3 tablespoons pignoli nuts (pine nuts)

❶ Preheat the oven to 350 degrees.

❷ Wash the grapes and discard stems. Dry grapes well and set aside.

❸ In a large bowl, whisk together the eggs, milk, ½ cup olive oil, vanilla, lemon zest, and ½ cup of the sugar. Blend thoroughly. Stir in the flour and mix well until smooth.

❹ Use 1 tablespoon oil to grease an 8-inch pie tin with a removable bottom and pour in the batter. Place the grapes evenly, about ¼ inch apart, in concentric circles on top of the batter to cover the entire surface. Press the grapes halfway into the batter. Scatter pignoli nuts evenly on the cake and sprinkle with 1 tablespoon of sugar. Bake for 45 minutes, until golden and firm to the touch. Remove from the oven and cool.

"It was so incredibly easy, but then it came out of the oven and looked like it could be served at a five-star restaurant. It was gorgeous!"

DANIELLE

"PINK FLAMINGO" YOGURT SMOOTHIE

The name says it all. Slightly tropical with a combination of sweet strawberries and luscious mango, the result is as pink as a flamingo. A great way to start the day, or delicious as an afternoon snack. ▷ **SERVES 4**

1 large ripe mango

12 ounces strawberries

1 cup plain low-fat yogurt

½ cup milk

¼ cup honey

❶ Prepare the mango (see sidebar) to get 1 heaping cup of diced fruit. Rinse the strawberries in a colander. Cut the green tops off all but 4 small berries (set these aside for later). Cut the berries in half.

❷ Put the strawberries and diced mango in a blender. Add the yogurt, milk, honey, and 8 ice cubes and process on high until the mixture is very smooth and thick. Pour into glasses and stick a strawberry on the rim of each glass.

HOW TO DEAL WITH A MANGO

Mangoes have a very large flat seed, so they cannot be sliced through the center. Grasp one side of the mango with the stem on top and slice down on the opposite side, cutting right next to the seed. Now do the same on the other side. Using your paring knife, carefully cut a ½-inch crosshatch pattern through the mango pulp down to the skin, being careful not to cut through the skin. Scoop out the flesh with a spoon. Scrape as much flesh as you can from the skin. Dice the flesh into small pieces; you will get about 1 heaping cup.

SUPER DRINK

PINEAPPLE-COCONUT FRULLATO

This super drink thickens as it sits in the fridge. Dairy-free, its creaminess comes from coconut milk.

▷ **SERVES 4**

1 medium very ripe pineapple

1 cup light coconut milk

¼ cup orange juice or apple juice

3 tablespoons honey

1 medium ripe banana

Carefully peel the pineapple, using a small sharp knife, keeping your fingers well back from the knife—it's slippery! Cut in half lengthwise and remove the core. Chop enough to get 3 packed cups. Or buy 12 ounces fresh-cut pineapple. Put the pineapple and any juices in a blender. Add the coconut milk, orange or apple juice, and honey. Peel the banana and cut it into pieces. Add to the blender with 8 ice cubes. Blend until the mixture is very smooth and thick. Serve immediately or cover and refrigerate until very cold.

CHAPTER 2 → → BOWLS: SOUPS & PASTA

juicy red gazpacho ▷ 36
SIDEBAR: TOPPINGS FOR GAZPACHO 36

"compost" vegetable broth ▷ 37
SIDEBAR: CORNCOB BROTH 37

very fresh vegetable soup ▷ 38
SIDEBAR: PESTO PRESTO 38

carrot-ginger-tomato soup ▷ 40
SIDEBAR: FRIED CARROT TOPS 40

onion soup with apple cider and thyme ▷ 42

risi e bisi ▷ 43

a word about pasta ▷ 44

summer/winter tomato sauce ▷ 45

"straw-and-hay" with uncooked tomato sauce ▷ 46

pasta primavera with jade zucchini sauce ▷ 48

bow ties with wilted tomatoes, spinach, and feta ▷ 49

lemony whole-wheat ziti with broccoli, parsnips, and prosciutto ▷ 50

spicy sesame noodles with crunchy snow peas ▷ 51

mac-and-cheese with cauliflower and creamy red pepper sauce ▷ 52

JUICY RED GAZPACHO

Gazpacho is a wonderful cold soup from Spain made from tomatoes, olive oil, and vinegar. Chefs blend in all kinds of interesting chopped vegetables for taste and texture, but in summer, I put chopped watermelon on top! ⇨ **SERVES 6**

½ **large bagel, lightly toasted**

¼ **cup olive oil**

1 **tablespoon sherry vinegar**

4 **large ripe plum tomatoes**

1 **large red bell pepper, seeded**

¼ **small yellow onion**

1 **large cucumber, peeled and seeded**

2 **cups tomato juice**

½ **teaspoon Tabasco sauce**

A **handful of fresh basil**

Tear the bagel into small pieces and put in the bowl of a food processor. Add the olive oil and vinegar. Cut the tomatoes, bell pepper, onion, and cucumber into pieces. Add to the food processor. Process until coarsely ground. Add the tomato juice and process until fairly smooth but still with a slightly chunky texture, adding up to 1 cup cold water to loosen. Season with Tabasco and add salt to taste. Cover and refrigerate for 2 hours. Ladle into soup bowls and garnish with slivers of fresh basil or any of the suggested toppings.

TOPPINGS FOR GAZPACHO

Chopped avocado

Tiny croutons

Finely diced yellow bell pepper

Chopped scallions or onions

Chopped cucumber

Dollop of thick yogurt

Chopped smoked almonds

Diced ripe watermelon, red or yellow

Add your own ideas!

"COMPOST" VEGETABLE BROTH

I love thinking of this soup as compost, for it is made with whatever vegetables you have lurking in your fridge: those scallion greens in the back of the bin; an ignored parsnip; a few scraggly carrots; and those overlooked flavor-boosters, the stems of fresh herbs—all coalesce to enrich a pot of water. ➪ **MAKES 6½ CUPS**

For example:

1 cup dried chickpeas

1 fresh bay leaf or 8 sprigs of fresh thyme

2 onions, unpeeled and halved

2 large carrots, peeled and quartered

1 tomato, quartered

2 large garlic cloves, smashed

1 celery rib with leaves, cut in pieces

¼ cup fresh basil or dill

1 slice of peeled fresh ginger

1 strip of lemon zest

Put all of the ingredients in a 4-quart pot. Add 10 cups cold water. Bring to a rapid boil. Lower the heat, adjusting it from time to time to maintain a simmer. Cover the pot and cook for 2 hours, or until the chickpeas are very soft. Strain through a wire strainer into a clean bowl. Add salt to taste.

CORNCOB BROTH

Here's another idea for recycling fresh ingredients: when using freshly cut corn from the cob, use the cobs instead of throwing them away! My faintly sweet corncob broth freezes well and can add a jolt of summer to soups and stews all year long. Sometimes we drink it instead of tea.

3 large ears of fresh corn

Husk the corn and remove the silk. Using a small sharp knife, remove the corn kernels from the cobs. Save the corn for another use. Break the cobs in half and put in a pot large enough to hold them in one layer. Cover with water by 1 inch, about 6 cups. Bring to a boil. Lower the heat and simmer, covered, for 20 minutes. Strain the broth through a wire strainer into a clean bowl. Add salt to taste.

MAKES ABOUT 1 QUART

VERY FRESH VEGETABLE SOUP

Sous-chef Danielle Hartog and her team said this was the best soup they had ever tasted. It is the essence of this book: a bushelful of freshness and goodness that comes together magically. Every ingredient can be found in a farmers' market, except the broth (or you can make the soup with water). During summer, use beefsteak tomatoes; in winter, a fourteen-ounce can of imported diced tomatoes will do nicely. A dollop of your own homemade pesto (see sidebar) is a delicious super-fresh touch. ▷ **SERVES 8**

3 tablespoons olive oil

2 cups diced red onion

2 cups diced butternut squash

1 cup diced fresh fennel

1 parsnip, peeled and diced

2 large garlic cloves, minced

2 teaspoons chopped fresh rosemary

2 large ripe tomatoes

6 cups chicken or vegetable broth

1 large zucchini, peeled and diced

5 cups firmly packed baby spinach, about 7 ounces

❶ Heat the oil over medium-high heat in a 6-quart pot. Add the onions, squash, fennel, parsnip, and 1 teaspoon salt. Cook, stirring frequently, until the vegetables begin to soften, about 10 minutes. Stir in the garlic and rosemary and cook for 2 more minutes.

❷ If using fresh tomatoes, dice them into small pieces; if using canned tomatoes, drain them (and discard the liquid or save it for another use).

❸ Stir the tomatoes and broth into the pot and bring to a boil. Lower the heat to medium and cook for 10 minutes. Stir in the zucchini, return the soup to a simmer, and cook for 10 minutes or until the zucchini is tender. Remove from the heat and stir in the spinach until wilted. Season with salt and pepper.

"The soup was so satisfying, but also very light. You could just feel all the vitamins rushing into you!"

DANIELLE

PESTO PRESTO

1 or 2 large bunches of fresh basil

⅓ cup freshly grated Parmesan

1 large garlic clove

6 tablespoons olive oil

2 tablespoons pignoli (pine nuts) or sliced almonds

Remove the basil leaves from the stems to get 2 packed cups. Wash the leaves and dry thoroughly. Put in a food processor or blender with the remaining ingredients. Process until just smooth. Add salt to taste.

MAKES ABOUT 1 CUP

CARROT-GINGER-TOMATo SOUP

While carrot-ginger soups have become commonplace, this one, enlivened with tomato, tastes a bit mysterious and especially fabulous. Fresh ginger adds a background of "heat" and flavor. I top it with crispy wisps of fried carrot tops! (see sidebar) ⟹ **SERVES 4 (MAKES 5 CUPS)**

1 large bunch of fresh carrots with green tops, about 12 ounces carrots

1 large baking potato, about 8 ounces

3 large garlic cloves, peeled

2 tablespoons chopped fresh ginger

2 large shallots, peeled and chopped

½ cup tomato sauce or tomato puree

2 tablespoons unsalted butter

❶ Peel the carrots (saving the green tops for later) and the potato. Cut into 1-inch pieces and put in a 3-quart pot. Add garlic cloves, ginger, and shallots.

Add 4 cups of water and ½ teaspoon salt. Bring to a rapid boil. Lower the heat to medium and cover. Cook 30 minutes, or until vegetables are very soft.

❷ Using a slotted spoon, transfer the vegetables to a food processor with half of the cooking liquid. Blend until smooth, slowly adding the remaining cooking liquid. Process until very smooth and add the tomato sauce and the butter. Return to the saucepan and bring to a simmer. Simmer for 10 minutes. Add salt and pepper to taste. Garnish with fried carrot tops!

FRIED CARROT TOPS

¼ cup lacy green carrot tops

3 tablespoons olive oil

Wash the carrot tops and dry thoroughly. Heat the oil in a small skillet until hot. Carefully add the carrot tops and fry for 30 seconds, or until crispy and still bright green. Transfer to paper towels. Sprinkle very lightly with salt. Stays crispy for several hours.

40

ONION SOUP
WITH APPLE CIDER AND THYME

This may become your favorite onion soup, even without the oozing cheese that blankets most versions. Here the onions are deeply caramelized until golden and sweet. The delicious broth gets its acidity and special flavor from fresh unpasteurized apple cider and a touch of thyme. ▷ **SERVES 6**

5 large onions, about 1½ pounds

2 tablespoons unsalted butter

1½ tablespoons olive oil

1½ cups organic chicken broth

1¼ cups fresh apple cider

1 bunch of fresh thyme

½ cup freshly grated Parmesan

❶ Peel the onions and cut them in half through the root end. Place them flat side down on a cutting board. Cut into thin slices (about ⅛ inch thick).

❷ Put the butter and oil in a 4-quart pot over medium heat. When the butter has melted, add the onions, increase the heat to high, and cook them, stirring frequently, for 10 minutes, or until they soften and get very dark brown and caramelized. Add the broth and cider, scraping up the browned bits in the pan, and bring to a boil.

❸ Lower the heat, and add 5 long sprigs of thyme and salt and pepper to taste. Cook over medium heat, uncovered, for 25 minutes, stirring often. Remove the thyme sprigs. Garnish with fresh thyme leaves and a sprinkling of the cheese.

RISI E BISI

This is what teenagers in northern Italy think of as comfort food. It literally means rice and peas, and the dish comes out a little soupy. I like to use a colorful combo of peas *and* sweet corn, cut from the cob. Make it your own by adding as many of the vibrant garnishes as you wish from the list below. ⟶ **SERVES 4**

¾ **cup shelled green peas**

¾ **cup fresh corn kernels**

3 large garlic cloves

1½ **tablespoons olive oil**

1 cup uncooked Arborio rice

½ **cup freshly grated Parmesan**

GARNISHES

Freshly grated lemon zest
Snipped fresh chives
Chopped fresh oregano
Red pepper flakes

❶ Bring a medium saucepan of salted water to a boil. Add the peas and cook for 5 minutes until just tender; add the corn and cook for 3 minutes longer. Drain well and set aside.

❷ Peel the garlic and chop fine. Heat the oil in a 4-quart pot. Add the garlic to the oil and cook for 1 minute, stirring constantly. Do not brown. Add the rice and stir for 1 minute. Add 4 cups water and bring to a boil. Lower the heat to medium-high and cook until the rice is just tender, about 18 minutes, stirring often.

❸ Add the peas and corn and cook for 3 minutes. Add the Parmesan cheese, along with salt and pepper to taste. Cook for 2 minutes longer, or until the rice is thick and creamy. Pour into 4 warm soup plates. Sprinkle each with the garnishes of your choice and serve.

A WORD ABOUT ▷ PASTA

It's easy to embellish a box of good-quality dried pasta by adding several cups of raw vegetables to the cooking water while the pasta magically transforms itself from something brittle and inedible to something tender. The vegetables augment a 2-ounce portion of pasta into a very generous serving.

Bring a large pot of salted water to a boil. Add 8 ounces of dried pasta and cook for 5 minutes. Then add 2 cups of diced carrots; or 5 cups of small broccoli or cauliflower florets; or 1 pint of small Brussels sprouts, cut in half; or 3 cups of diced winter squash; or 1½ cups of blanched green peas; or 4 ounces of haricots verts (thin string beans) or string beans you have trimmed and cut in half, lengthwise (this is known as "frenching"); or 1 cup of fresh corn kernels; or a combination of the above. Cook the vegetables for the last 8 minutes of boiling the pasta. Drain well and serve 4 hungry friends.

All will taste delicious with a ladleful of one of the following tomato sauces. One sauce features ripe red tomatoes in season; the other utilizes the best-quality canned plum tomatoes, San Marzano (if you can find them), which great Italian chefs use most often. Each recipe "dresses" four portions of pasta. Dust with grated Parmesan or Asiago cheese, or with the more strongly flavored Pecorino. Our teen friends also enjoy shaking red pepper flakes (affectionately known as "razors") on top!

SUMMER
TOMATO SAUCE

Make this simple sauce when plum (also known as Roma), beefsteak, or heirloom tomatoes are at their peak.

▷ **MAKES ABOUT 2 CUPS**

2 tablespoons olive oil

2 large garlic cloves

½ cup finely diced onion

2 pounds very ripe tomatoes

4 large fresh basil leaves

Put the oil in a heavy medium saucepan. Peel the garlic and chop very fine. Add the garlic and onion to the saucepan. Cook over medium-high heat until the onion softens but does not brown, about 3 minutes. Add the tomatoes and bring to a boil. Add the basil and cook, covered, over medium heat for 10 minutes. Pass through a food mill or process briefly in a food processor. Add salt, pepper, and a pinch of sugar, if needed, to taste.

WINTER
TOMATO SAUCE

This is our favorite tomato sauce enhanced with lemon, ginger, and honey. We keep a large jar in the fridge (it lasts for several days) for tossing with pasta, drizzling over grilled chicken, or pouring atop baked spaghetti squash. You get the idea!

▷ **MAKES 2 CUPS**

28 ounces canned organic whole tomatoes in puree

3 large garlic cloves, peeled

1 lemon slice, about ¼ inch thick, seeds removed

2 nickel-size pieces of peeled fresh ginger

1 teaspoon dried oregano leaves

1 tablespoon honey

2 tablespoons olive oil

Put all the ingredients in the bowl of a food processor and process until very smooth. Transfer to a large saucepan. Bring to a boil over high heat. Boil for 1 minute, then lower the heat to medium and cook for 10 to 15 minutes, stirring often, until thick. Add salt to taste.

"Cooking is like doing a lab experiment, only you get to eat the results!"

IAN

"STRAW-AND-HAY" WITH UNCOOKED TOMATO SAUCE

This fabulous sauce is made from uncooked tomatoes that marinate for several hours. Its beautiful flavor and aroma are released when it is tossed with steaming pasta. I like to use *paglia-e-fieno* or "straw-and-hay" pasta, which is an Italian combo of white and green (spinach) fettuccine and looks really pretty. ⟹ **SERVES 4**

1½ **pounds ripe heirloom tomatoes**

1 **small garlic clove, finely minced**

5 **tablespoons extra-virgin olive oil**

2 **tablespoons minced red onion**

½ **cup finely slivered fresh basil**

8 **ounces dried straw-and-hay pasta**

⅔ **cup freshly grated Parmesan**

❶ Cut the tomatoes into ½-inch pieces and place in a jar with a lid (or in a large bowl). Add the garlic, 3 table-spoons of the olive oil, the red onion, and half of the basil. Add salt to taste. Stir and cover the jar. Let sit 2 hours.

❷ Bring a large pot of salted water to a boil. Add the pasta and cook for 12 minutes, or until just tender. Carefully drain in a colander and immediately transfer to a large bowl. Toss with the tomato mixture, ½ cup of the cheese, and the remaining 2 tablespoons olive oil. Add salt to taste. Scatter the remaining cheese and basil on top.

PASTA PRIMAVERA
WITH JADE ZUCCHINI SAUCE

Primavera means "spring" in Italian and describes the taste of this colorful dish, no matter what season you make it. The unusual, rich-tasting jade-green sauce is made from fresh zucchini that gets boiled and pureed with a bit of sweet butter. You can add some fresh asparagus tips to the pasta in spring and bits of butternut squash in winter. It will be delicious hot, cold, or in between. ▷ **SERVES 4**

3 medium zucchini, about 6 ounces each

2 large garlic cloves, peeled

4 large fresh basil leaves

1½ tablespoons unsalted butter

3 bell peppers: 1 each red, yellow, orange

8 ounces dried cavatappi, cellentani, or fusilli pasta

1 tablespoon olive oil

½ cup freshly grated Parmesan

❶ Wash the zucchini and pat dry. Trim the ends. Cut 1½ of the zucchini into 1-inch pieces. Put in a small saucepan with ¾ cup water. Cut the garlic in half lengthwise. Add to the saucepan with a large pinch of salt. Bring to a boil over medium-high heat, then cook, covered, for 15 minutes, or until the zucchini is very soft. Transfer the contents of the saucepan to a food processor; add the basil and butter and process until very smooth. This is the jade sauce.

❷ Cut the remaining zucchini into ¼-inch dice. Cut the bell peppers in half, remove the seeds, and cut into thin strips. Bring a large pot of salted water to a rapid boil. Add the pasta and bell peppers. Bring back to a boil and cook for 10 minutes. Add the zucchini and cook for 2 minutes longer. Drain well in a colander. Transfer to a large bowl and toss with the olive oil. Pour the sauce over pasta and vegetables and sprinkle with the cheese.

BOW TIES WITH WILTED TOMATOES, SPINACH, AND FETA

Great flavors: feta cheese, tomatoes, and slightly bitter baby spinach flecked with a bit of orange zest. If the season allows, try yellow teardrop tomatoes instead of cherry tomatoes for a great look. Use bow-tie pasta, also known as farfalle.

▷ **SERVES 4**

8 ounces bow-tie pasta

6 scallions

3 tablespoons extra-virgin olive oil

3 large garlic cloves, minced

1 pint small cherry tomatoes

1 pint grape tomatoes

5 ounces baby spinach

1½ cups crumbled feta cheese

1 orange

❶ Bring a large pot of salted water to a boil. Add the pasta and cook for 10 minutes, or until just tender.

❷ Trim the scallions and chop enough of the white and green part to get 1 cup. Heat 2 tablespoons of the oil in a large, heavy skillet over high heat. Add the scallions, garlic, and tomatoes. Cook, stirring constantly, until the tomatoes collapse, about 7 minutes. Add salt and pepper to taste.

❸ Drain the pasta and return it to the pot it cooked in. Add the tomato mixture, spinach, and remaining oil. Toss until the spinach begins to wilt. Cook for 1 to 2 minutes, until hot. Remove from the heat. Stir in the feta. Add salt and pepper to taste. Divide among 4 warm bowls and dust with a little grated orange zest. Serve immediately.

LEMONY WHOLE-WHEAT ZITI
WITH BROCCOLI, PARSNIPS, AND PROSCIUTTO

It doesn't get much better, or simpler, than this. Bits of bright green broccoli and nuggets of sweet white parsnips add amazing flavor to whole-wheat pasta, either ziti or penne. Strips of slightly salty prosciutto add an impressive touch, but they are optional if you are vegetarian. ⮕ **SERVES 6**

2 medium parsnips

8 ounces dried whole-wheat ziti

6 cups small broccoli florets

2 tablespoons unsalted butter

2 tablespoons olive oil

1 large garlic clove

1 lemon

2 ounces thinly sliced prosciutto

⅓ cup freshly grated Parmesan

❶ Peel the parsnips and cut into ½-inch cubes. Bring a large pot of salted water to a boil. Add the pasta and parsnips and cook for 5 minutes. Add the broccoli and continue to boil for about 8 minutes, or until the pasta is cooked and the broccoli is tender, but still bright green.
❷ Meanwhile, combine the butter and olive oil in a large serving bowl. Peel the garlic and mince very fine. Add to the bowl. Grate the zest of the lemon

and squeeze the lemon to get 1 tablespoon juice. Add the zest and juice to the bowl. Set aside.
❸ Cut the prosciutto across the width into ½-inch-wide strips. Set aside.
❹ Drain the pasta and vegetables in a colander. Shake dry and add to the bowl with the butter. Add cheese and toss. Scatter the prosciutto on top and serve.

AMAZING FLAVOR

SPICY SESAME NOODLES WITH CRUNCHY SNOW PEAS

Asian sesame noodles are generally eaten cold but are also delicious hot, streaked with crunchy snow peas and carrot slivers. The sauce, which takes only minutes to prepare, is made bolder with sriracha, a spicy chili sauce from Thailand. Top with a tuft of pea shoots, if you can find some. ▷ **SERVES 4**

¼ **cup smooth peanut butter**

2 **tablespoons peeled chopped fresh ginger**

¼ **cup chopped scallions**

2 **tablespoons soy sauce**

1 **tablespoon dark Asian sesame oil**

1 **tablespoon rice vinegar**

1 **tablespoon honey**

1 **large garlic clove**

¼ **teaspoon sriracha or Tabasco sauce**

6 **ounces snow peas**

1 **large carrot, peeled**

8 **ounces linguine**

3 **tablespoons chopped fresh cilantro or mint or both**

❶ Combine peanut butter, ginger, scallions, soy sauce, sesame oil, vinegar, honey, garlic, and sriracha in the bowl of a food processor. Process, adding 2 tablespoons water, until smooth.

❷ Trim the snow peas and remove the strings running along the side. Cut the carrot into very thin julienned strips, about 2 inches long x ⅛ inch wide (like matchsticks).

❸ Bring a large pot of salted water to a boil. Add the linguine and boil for 10 minutes, or until just tender. Add the snow peas and carrots and cook for about 3 minutes longer, until just tender. Drain well and shake dry. Transfer the pasta and vegetables to a large bowl and toss with the sauce. Top with the cilantro or mint and serve.

"I always make things spicy, to see how hot I can take it."

DAN

MAC-AND-CHEESE
WITH CAULIFLOWER AND CREAMY RED PEPPER SAUCE

This is an unusual macaroni and cheese, studded with surprise nuggets of cauliflower. The gorgeous bright orange sauce is made from cooked red bell peppers and garlic that get pureed together until silky. My daughter and her friends like making it because it looks like it's oozing with cheese, but it has much less fat and is more nutritious than regular mac-and-cheese. ➪ **SERVES 6**

4 ounces very sharp yellow cheddar cheese

2 medium red bell peppers, about 12 ounces

3 large garlic cloves, peeled

1 tablespoon unsalted butter

1 teaspoon honey

⅛ teaspoon chipotle chile powder

8 ounces ziti or penne rigate

5 cups small cauliflower florets

3 tablespoons finely chopped chives

❶ Shred the cheese on the large holes of a box grater and set aside.

❷ Cut the peppers in half and remove the seeds. Cut into 1-inch pieces and put in a small saucepan with ½ cup water. Cut the garlic in half, lengthwise, and add to the saucepan. Bring to a boil, lower the heat to medium, and cover. Cook for 15 minutes, or until the peppers are very soft. Transfer the contents of the saucepan, including the water, to a food processor or blender. Add the butter, honey, chile powder, and salt to taste and process until *very* smooth. Return to the saucepan.

❸ Meanwhile, bring a large pot of salted water to a boil. Add the pasta and cauliflower and cook for 12 minutes, or until tender. Drain well and shake dry. Transfer to a large bowl. Heat the sauce and pour it over the pasta. Add the cheese and stir well. Add salt to taste. Sprinkle with chives.

CHAPTER 3

SANDWICHES, BURGERS & PIZZA

avocado mayonnaise ⟫ 56

fun and delicious garnishes ⟫ 57

great fish tacos ⟫ 58

bbq onion and smoked gouda quesadilla ⟫ 60

bombay sliders with hurry-curry sauce ⟫ 61

chickpea burger with fresh mango salsa ⟫ 62
SIDEBAR: SRIRACHA KETCHUP 63

asian summer rolls, fun sauce ⟫ 64

pita fajita ⟫ 66

farmers' market pizza, baking powder crust ⟫ 69

AVOCADO MAYONNAISE

My pretty green mayonnaise tastes brighter than regular jarred mayo.
And it is better for you because unhealthy fats get replaced with the healthier
monounsaturated fats found in avocado. Every tablespoon has only 25 calories
instead of 100. ▷ **MAKES 2 ¼ CUPS**

1 ripe medium avocado, 8 ounces

1 scallion, white part only

1¾ cups buttermilk

½ tablespoon sugar

¼ cup olive oil

A few drops of hot sauce

1 lime

Cut the avocado in half, running your
knife around the large pit. Now twist
each half and the avocado will split
apart in 2 sections. Remove the pit with
a spoon. Scoop out the flesh and put
in a blender. Chop the scallion and
put in the blender with the buttermilk,
sugar, olive oil, and hot sauce. Cut lime
in half and squeeze 2 tablespoons juice
into the blender. Process until creamy.
Add salt to taste.

FUN AND DELICIOUS GARNISHES

GRAPE TOMATO SKEWERS

4 6-inch bamboo skewers

24 grape tomatoes

Thread 6 grape tomatoes on each bamboo skewer.

MAKES 4

RAW CARROT "FRIES"

1 pound fresh carrots, orange or red

Peel the carrots and cut into "fry" shapes using a crinkle-cutter if possible.

SERVES 6

CARROT CURLS

3 very large carrots

Peel the carrots. Using a sharp vegetable peeler with a horizontal blade, remove long strips of carrot, running the length of the carrot. Dig deeply into the carrot. Roll each long strip around your finger. Secure with a toothpick. Put the rolled carrots into a deep container and cover with cold water. Refrigerate for several hours so that the carrots crisp up. Remove the toothpicks and unravel the carrots.

**MAKES ABOUT 30
(8 TO 10 PER CARROT)
SERVES 6**

GRAPE CLUSTERS

12 ounces seedless red or green grapes on the stem

Wash the grapes and dry well. Using a grape scissors or small knife, cut into small clusters. You should have 3 ounces per person.

SERVES 4

COOL CUKES

These are tart, cool, and refreshing, and they make a great side dish for any sandwich.

2 large cucumbers

2 limes

¼ cup finely minced red bell pepper

¼ cup finely julienned fresh cilantro

1 tablespoon olive oil

Peel the cucumbers. Slice them paper thin and put in a large bowl. Cut the limes in half and squeeze their juice over the cucumbers. Stir in the bell peppers, cilantro, and oil. Add salt to taste. Chill for 30 minutes.

SERVES 4

FRESH HERBS

Garnish sandwiches with sprigs of fresh basil, mint, parsley, or rosemary.

GREAT FISH TACOS

An improv "taco bar" is a great way to get your friends and family involved in making their own mouthwatering meal. Use any firm white fish, such as halibut, flounder, or tilapia. If you like seared rare tuna, then try that! Fixings for the taco bar could include lettuce or cabbage, avocado, red onion, cilantro, and bell peppers. Be as creative, and seasonal, as you wish. ▷ **SERVES 4 TO 8**

for the tacos

2 tablespoons olive oil

1 teaspoon ground cumin

1 teaspoon ground coriander

½ teaspoon chili powder

1 small garlic clove

1½ pounds halibut fillets

8 6-inch corn tortillas

for the taco bar

2 cups shredded green or red cabbage

¾ cup chopped onion

1 cup chopped fresh tomato

1 cup diced avocado

½ cup fresh cilantro leaves

½ cup Avocado Mayonnaise (see page 56)

8 lime wedges

❶ Combine the olive oil, cumin, coriander, chili powder, and ¼ teaspoon salt, in a medium bowl. Push garlic through a press and add to bowl. Cut the fish into 1-inch strips. Toss the fish in the spice mixture to coat. Set aside while you warm the tortillas.

❷ Heat an 8-inch skillet over medium heat for 3 minutes. One at a time, crisp the tortillas on each side for about 30 seconds. Fold gently and set aside.

❸ In a large nonstick skillet, cook the fish over medium-high heat for 2 to 3 minutes on each side until opaque and flaky. Transfer to a large plate and break the fish into large chunks.

❹ To assemble the tacos: Put the shredded cabbage in a crisp tortilla and fill it with fish and other fixings. Finish with a dollop of Avocado Mayonnaise and a squeeze of fresh lime juice.

BBQ ONION AND SMOKED GOUDA
QUESADILLA

I adore this combination of flavors, made with smoky barbecue sauce or dark black hoisin (Chinese barbecue sauce). The filling tastes so meaty that it's hard to believe it's vegetarian. If you want to be daring, substitute chopped fresh pineapple for the diced tomatoes. Serve with a green salad. ⇨ **SERVES 8**

2 large yellow onions

5 tablespoons olive oil

⅓ cup barbecue or hoisin sauce

8 8-inch flour tortillas

8 ounces smoked Gouda cheese, shredded

⅓ cup julienned fresh basil or cilantro

4 large plum tomatoes, diced

❶ Preheat the oven to 300 degrees.
❷ Peel the onions, cut them in half, and then cut into thin half-rings. Put 3 tablespoons of the oil in a large non-stick skillet. Add the onions; cook over high heat, stirring, for 4 minutes, or until soft. Lower the heat, add the barbecue sauce and 2 tablespoons water, and cook for 2 minutes longer.

❸ Place 4 of the tortillas on a large flat surface. Sprinkle half of each tortilla evenly with cheese, basil or cilantro, cooked onions, and diced tomatoes (or pineapple!) and fold over. Press lightly. Heat a teaspoon of oil in a large skillet and cook each quesadilla for about 2 minutes on each side. Repeat with the remaining tortillas and filling. Place on a baking sheet in the oven until all are cooked.

"I love cooking in my kitchen. When I'm alone in there, I can really think about flavors and create wonderful foods, but I also like when my friends and I get together to cook. It always feels like a party."

. . . .

ROBYN

BOMBAY SLIDERS
WITH HURRY-CURRY SAUCE

These little burgers are fun to eat. You'll want to slather the sauce on everything except dessert. From the farmers' market, you'll need fresh scallions, cilantro or basil, kirby cucumbers, and ripe plum tomatoes. ➪ **SERVES 4 TO 6**

hurry-curry sauce

½ cup light mayonnaise

⅔ cup plain yogurt

1 tablespoon curry powder

2 tablespoons ketchup

1 small garlic clove

sliders

2 pounds ground turkey

4 teaspoons curry powder

2 teaspoons ground cumin

¾ teaspoon hot chili powder

¼ cup finely minced scallions

6 tablespoons finely chopped
   fresh cilantro or basil

2-inch piece of peeled fresh ginger,
   finely minced

¼ cup light mayonnaise

1 tablespoon olive oil

12 little dinner rolls, split and toasted

12 thin slices of kirby cucumber

12 thin slices of plum tomato

❶ Put first four ingredients for the curry sauce in a bowl. Add garlic, pushed through a press. Stir, cover, and refrigerate.

❷ Put the ground turkey in a large bowl. Add the curry, cumin, chili powder, scallions, cilantro, ginger, and mayo, plus 1 teaspoon salt. Mix until blended; do not overmix or the mixture will get mushy. Form the mixture into 12 little burgers. ❸ Heat the olive oil in a large nonstick skillet and cook the burgers over medium-high heat for 2 minutes; turn over and cook 2 minutes longer. Place the burgers on the buns and slather with curry sauce. Top with a slice of cucumber and tomato.

FUN TO EAT

CHICKPEA BURGER WITH FRESH MANGO SALSA

Ground-up chickpeas have a "meaty" mouthfeel and taste great as a "burger." Fresh mango salsa adds juicy flavor. If you want to add a drizzle of ketchup, make it special by adding spicy sriracha sauce (see sidebar). You may substitute plain bread crumbs, but I prefer panko, or Japanese bread crumbs, which are available in most supermarkets. ▷ **SERVES 4**

fresh mango salsa

1 cup finely diced ripe mango (see page 30) or ripe peaches

1 tablespoon finely chopped scallion

2 tablespoons minced red bell pepper

2 tablespoons slivered fresh cilantro or basil

½ teaspoon ground cumin

Freshly squeezed lime juice, to taste

burger

1¾ cups canned chickpeas, rinsed and drained

¾ cup panko (Japanese bread crumbs)

1 extra-large egg

1 large zucchini, about 6 ounces, grated and squeezed dry

½ cup grated carrots

1 scallion, cut into 1-inch pieces

1 teaspoon ground cumin

3 tablespoons olive oil

4 sections of French bread or English muffins, toasted

4 curly-leaf lettuce leaves

❶ Put all the salsa ingredients in a medium bowl. Add salt to taste. Stir and set aside.

❷ Preheat the oven to 425 degrees. Put the first 7 ingredients for the burgers in the bowl of a food processor with 2 tablespoons of the olive oil and 1 teaspoon salt. Process until just smooth. Form into 4 thick patties. Cover and refrigerate until ready to cook.

❸ Drizzle about ½ teaspoon oil on each side of the burgers. Place them on a rimmed baking sheet, several inches apart. Bake for 8 minutes, turn over with a spatula, and bake for 8 minutes longer, or until golden and crispy. Put a leaf of lettuce on each piece of toasted bread. Top with chickpea burger and add ¼ cup of the salsa. If you wish, drizzle with sriracha ketchup. Cover with the top piece of bread or eat it open-faced.

SPICY!

SRIRACHA KETCHUP

Before you can say "sriracha," you can whip up a spicy sauce that will tickle your taste buds.

½ cup ketchup

½ teaspoon sriracha hot sauce

Stir the ketchup and sriracha together in a small bowl.

MAKES ½ CUP

ASIAN SUMMER ROLLS, FUN SAUCE

I think of these authentic Vietnamese summer rolls as "see-through sandwiches" because you can see the filling through the wrapper, which is made of rice paper. You can find the hard round rice-paper disks in the Asian section of your supermarket or in many specialty food shops. You dip them in water to soften them, which is part of the fun. You can add cooked rice noodles, chilled shrimp, shredded chicken, or anything else fresh from the farmers' market. My "fun sauce" also makes a great marinade for chicken or steak. ▷ **SERVES 8**

fun sauce

2 scallions

6 tablespoons rice vinegar

6 tablespoons soy sauce

2 teaspoons dark Asian sesame oil

2 tablespoons honey

2 teaspoons peeled fresh ginger, finely minced

summer rolls

8 8-inch rice-paper rounds

8 Boston lettuce leaves

1½ cups alfalfa or bean sprouts

1 cup rice noodles, boiled, drained, and chilled

1 cup finely julienned cucumber strips

1 cup finely julienned carrot strips

1 cup julienned red bell pepper strips

16 thin slices of ripe avocado

16 ultra-thin slices of ripe mango (see page 30)

16 fresh mint leaves

❶ To make the sauce, trim the scallions and finely mince to get ¼ cup. Put in a small bowl. Add the remaining ingredients plus 2 tablespoons of water. Whisk until smooth. Makes about 1 cup.

❷ For the rolls, put 1 inch of warm water in a large, shallow bowl. Soak a rice-paper round for about 30 seconds, until soft. Then lift carefully from the water and let the moisture drain off. Place the softened rice paper on a clean kitchen towel or other flat surface.

❸ Place a lettuce leaf onto the center of the rice paper. Equally divide and spread out on each lettuce leaf some sprouts; cooked rice noodles; a few cucumber strips, carrot strips, and bell pepper strips; 2 slices of avocado; 2 slices of mango; and 2 mint leaves.

❹ Fold the sides of the rice paper toward the center, fold the bottom edge of the rice paper over the vegetables, and roll up. Repeat with the remaining ingredients.

❺ Place each roll seam side down on a serving platter. Cover with a damp kitchen towel so that they don't dry out. Cut rolls in half before serving. Dip into fun sauce.

> "It is amazing how easy and fun it can be to cook foods I thought I would only be able to order in restaurants. Following these recipes made it easy. It is fun to see how a table full of ingredients can be transformed into meals that we prepared."
>
> • • • • • • • •
> **IAN**

PITA FAJITA

This is a combo of two of my favorite sandwiches: I drizzle tahini sauce, generally used in Middle Eastern falafel sandwiches, over a filling of spicy Mexican steak fajitas stuffed in a pita pocket. But you can also roll this zingy filling into leaves of Bibb or Boston lettuce. Tahini, or sesame seed paste, looks like peanut butter and can be found in most supermarkets. ⇨ **SERVES 4**

¼ **cup tahini**

¼ **cup plus 2 tablespoons freshly squeezed lime juice**

4 small garlic cloves

1 pound skirt steak

1½ teaspoons ground cumin

3 tablespoons olive oil

3 bell peppers: 1 red, 1 orange, 1 yellow

1 medium red onion, peeled

4 pita breads with pockets

4 romaine lettuce leaves, shredded

1 tomato, finely chopped

❶ In a small bowl, whisk together the tahini, 2 tablespoons of the lime juice, and 1 garlic clove pushed through a press. Whisk in ¼ cup water and stir until very smooth. Set aside.

❷ Put the steak in a large bowl. In a small bowl, whisk together the remaining ¼ cup lime juice, 3 garlic cloves pushed through a press, cumin, and 2 tablespoons of the olive oil. Pour over the steak and let it marinate, covered and chilled, for 1 hour.

❸ Wash and dry the peppers. Cut them in half and remove the seeds. Cut them into thin strips. Cut the onion in half through the root end, then cut it into thin half circles.

❹ Heat the remaining tablespoon of oil in a large skillet. Add the bell peppers and onion and cook for 5 minutes over high heat. Add the steak and cook until seared, about 2 minutes on each side. Remove the steak and cut into thin strips across the width. Combine meat in a bowl with the peppers and onions.

❺ Warm each pita directly on the stove, turning over an open flame quickly with tongs. Cut each pita pocket in half and put in lettuce, tomato, then steak and peppers. Drizzle tahini sauce over the filling.

ZINGY!

FARMERS' MARKET PIZZA, BAKING POWDER CRUST

The pastry crust of this fantastic pizza holds up all day long without getting soggy. It's good hot, warm, or even cold from the fridge for breakfast. Why not? It's healthy! Use your own homemade tomato sauce or buy a good brand. The team thought it was awesome to make and felt proud to serve it! ▷ **SERVES 6 TO 8**

pizza crust

2 cups all-purpose flour, plus more for dusting the counter

2 teaspoons baking powder

⅓ cup olive oil

¾ cup milk

topping

1¼ cups homemade tomato sauce (see page 45) or store-bought

1 medium zucchini, sliced very thin

1 yellow squash, sliced very thin

¾ cup sliced grape tomatoes

¾ cup diced yellow bell pepper

2 scallions, finely chopped

3 tablespoons fresh oregano leaves

4 ounces shredded Asiago cheese

❶ In a medium bowl, mix the flour, baking powder, and 1 teaspoon salt. Make a well in the center. Pour the olive oil and milk into a large measuring cup and stir. Pour the mixture into the well of the flour. Stir with a wooden spoon until the ingredients are blended and a smooth dough is formed.

❷ Lightly flour your counter. Roll out the dough into a ⅛-inch-thick rectangle about 10 x 13 inches. Gently transfer to an ungreased, rimmed baking sheet, pressing the dough down to again form a 10 x 13-inch rectangle. (The dough will be a bit spongy at this point and will start to shrink back.) Using the tines of a fork, pierce the dough all over at 1-inch intervals. Let the dough rest while you preheat the oven to 425 degrees.

❸ Smooth the tomato sauce over the crust, leaving a ¼-inch border all around. Cover evenly with slices of zucchini and yellow squash. Add the grape tomatoes, yellow pepper, scallions, and oregano. Sprinkle cheese evenly on top. Bake 22 minutes, until the cheese has melted, and the edges of the crust are golden brown.

"The best times are when my friends get together, play our favorite music really loud, and cook some of our favorite food."

IAN

guacamole with jicama pick-up sticks ⇨ 72

peanut butter hummus with crudités ⇨ 73
SIDEBAR: IDEAS FOR CRUDITÉS 73

create-your-own seasonal "house" salad ⇨ 74

great salad dressings ⇨ 76

pink pickled onions ⇨ 77

eggless caesar with toasted pecans, green apple "croutons" ⇨ 78
SIDEBAR: HOW TO TOAST PECANS 78
SIDEBAR: PROSCIUTTO "CHOPSTICKS" 78

endive salad with fancy greens, walnuts and cranberries,
maple vinaigrette, and turkey "pasta" ⇨ 80

warm lemon-cumin chicken on pita bread salad ⇨ 83

tuna-pasta niçoise with sweet peas ⇨ 85
SIDEBAR: HOW TO MAKE A PERFECT BOILED EGG 85

overnight vegetable tabbouleh ⇨ 86

string bean salad with fresh tomato chutney ⇨ 87

sloppy slaw with carrot-ginger dressing ⇨ 88

GUACAMOLE WITH JICAMA PICK-UP STICKS

Avocados are a good source of healthy fats, which is a great reason for loving guacamole. You'll find jicama—pronounced hee-kah-mah—in a good produce market. It is a big crunchy tuber, larger than a softball, that is juicy and mildly sweet. ⊳ **SERVES 4**

2 large ripe avocados

3 limes, plus more if needed

¼ cup finely minced red onion

1 tablespoon finely minced jalapeño pepper or hot sauce to taste

1 teaspoon ground cumin

2 plum tomatoes, finely diced

¼ cup chopped fresh cilantro

1 jicama, about 1 pound

2 teaspoons chili powder

❶ Cut the avocados in half, navigating around the pit. Remove the pit with a spoon. Scoop out the flesh and put in a large bowl. Mash well with the juice of 2 of the limes. Add the onion, jalapeño, and cumin. Add salt to taste and additional lime juice if needed to get the flavor you like. Stir in diced tomatoes. Transfer to a bowl and sprinkle with the cilantro. Cover and refrigerate.

❷ To prepare the jicama: Using a vegetable peeler or small sharp knife, peel the jicama. Cut into ¼-inch slices, then cut across into ¼-inch strips. They should look like French fries. Put in a bowl and squeeze in the juice of the remaining lime. Toss, add salt to taste, and sprinkle with the chili powder. Serve with the guacamole.

SAY: HEE-KAH-MAH

PEANUT BUTTER HUMMUS WITH CRUDITÉS

Making your own hummus (a Middle Eastern dip made from chickpeas) is lots more fun than buying it ready-made, and homemade tastes better, too. You can cook your own chickpeas (which takes hours), or use a nineteen-ounce can, drained in a colander, rinsed under cold water, and patted dry. Crudités? That's a French word for fresh-cut vegetables that are better than chips for dipping.

▷ **MAKES ABOUT 1 ¾ CUPS**

2 cups cooked or canned chickpeas

3 tablespoons creamy natural
    peanut butter

2 tablespoons freshly squeezed
    lemon juice

1 small garlic clove, peeled

1 tablespoon olive oil

1 teaspoon ground cumin

A splash of hot sauce

Put all ingredients in the bowl of a food processor. Add ½ teaspoon salt and ⅓ cup water. Process until very smooth. Add more hot sauce if desired.

IDEAS FOR CRUDITÉS

Carrot sticks

Zucchini rounds

Cucumber spears

Grape tomatoes on skewers

Halved radishes

Celery boats

Broccoli florets

Cauliflower florets

Sugar snap peas

Yellow wax beans

CREATE-YOUR-OWN SEASONAL "HOUSE" SALAD

You can turn any of your "house" salads into a main course by adding strips of juicy grilled chicken, fresh seared tuna, or steamed or roasted vegetables. This is the time to use your creativity and skills as a chef. Nature provides the rest of the inspiration. ⇨ **SERVES 6**

6 ounces mixed baby lettuces or mesclun

To make the salad: Put the mixed greens in a large bowl. Add your choice of mix-ins. Toss with enough dressing (see recipes on page 76) to just coat. Add salt and pepper to taste.

FALL

Add diced pears or julienned apples and shredded cheddar cheese; toasted almonds; Belgian endive, wedges of fresh figs, roasted grapes, and sliced mushrooms.

WINTER

Add grated carrots (1 medium carrot yields ½ cup grated); pickled onions (see page 77); shredded radicchio; pomegranate seeds; sliced or diced radishes, and orange or tangerine segments.

SPRING

Add quartered strawberries; grilled asparagus; spring onions; thinly sliced fennel; quickly cooked sugar snaps; julienned snow peas; watercress; Vidalia onions; chives.

SUMMER

Add sliced or shredded zucchini; thin slices of watermelon and feta cheese; julienned basil; diced peaches or nectarines, or thin wedges of plums; diced heirloom tomatoes; yellow cherry tomatoes; corn kernels cut from the cob; sliced kirby cucumbers.

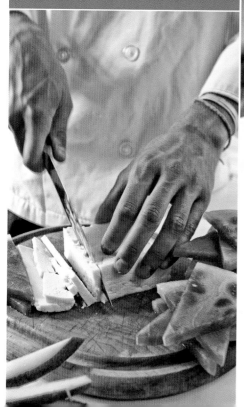

GREAT SALAD DRESSINGS

FRESH HERB VINAIGRETTE

2 tablespoons white wine vinegar

¾ cup vegetable oil

2 teaspoons Dijon mustard

2 teaspoons chopped fresh herbs such
    as basil, thyme, or flat-leaf parsley

Shake everything in a jar with a screw
lid. Add 2 tablespoons water, ½ teaspoon
salt, and ¼ teaspoon black pepper. Shake
again. Keeps in the fridge for 1 week.

MAKES ABOUT 1 CUP

LEMON-PARMESAN VINAIGRETTE

1 large lemon

3 tablespoons freshly grated Parmesan

1 teaspoon fresh thyme leaves

¼ cup olive oil

Grate the zest of the lemon and put
it in a small bowl. Squeeze the lemon
to get 1½ tablespoons of juice. Add to
the bowl with the cheese and thyme.
Whisk in the oil until creamy. Put in
a measuring cup. Add enough water
to make it ½ cup. Mix well. Add salt
and pepper to taste.

MAKES ½ CUP

MAPLE VINAIGRETTE
(page 80)

REAL FRENCH DRESSING

I used to love this thick orange-y (color, not flavor)
dressing as a kid. It was known as French dressing
or Catalina dressing and it came in bottles. This
homemade one has a similar style but is lighter
and fresh-tasting. It is especially delicious over
ripe tomatoes (and thinly sliced onions, if you like
them) and crumbles of blue cheese. Good, too,
just tossed with seasonal greens.

2 tablespoons apple cider vinegar

2 tablespoons honey

¼ cup ketchup

1 teaspoon Dijon mustard

⅓ cup olive oil

1 small garlic clove, pushed through a press

In a medium bowl, whisk together the vinegar
and honey until the honey dissolves. Whisk in the
ketchup, mustard, and oil until blended. Stir in
the garlic, 2 tablespoons water, and salt to taste.

MAKES ¾ CUP

BALSAMIC-ROSEMARY VINAIGRETTE

2 tablespoons good balsamic vinegar

¼ cup olive oil

½ small garlic clove

¼ teaspoon finely minced fresh rosemary

In a small bowl, whisk together the vinegar
and oil. Push the garlic through a
press and add. Whisk in the rosemary
and add salt and pepper to taste.

MAKES ⅓ CUP

PINK PICKLED
ONIONS

This may be one of our family's favorite extras and it dresses up everything. It's super on any salad, tucked in a sandwich, or piled on top of grilled chicken or burgers.

▷ **MAKES ABOUT 2 CUPS**

**4 medium red onions,
    about 1 pound**

1 cup rice vinegar

6 tablespoons raw (turbinado) sugar

2-inch sprig of fresh rosemary

Peel the onions and slice very thin. Place them in a large heat-proof jar with a cover. Put the vinegar, sugar, 1½ cups water, and 1 teaspoon salt in a large saucepan. Bring to a boil and boil for 2 minutes. Pour the mixture over the onions. Add the rosemary sprig. Let cool. Add more water to cover onions, if necessary. Cover and refrigerate for 1 day before using. Remove rosemary. Drain and pat dry before putting the onions on sandwiches or salads.

EGGLESS CAESAR WITH TOASTED PECANS, GREEN APPLE "CROUTONS"

My sous-chefs agreed that this was the simplest and tastiest Caesar around—because the dressing was light and airy as opposed to the gloppy dressings that have become associated with this salad. Instead of the usual anchovies, I snuck in a little Thai fish sauce (available in most supermarkets, in the Asian section). Granny Smith apples take the place of croutons. If you wish, place some Prosciutto "Chopsticks" (see sidebar) on top! ➪ **SERVES 6**

dressing

½ cup olive oil

1 small garlic clove, pushed through a press or minced

2 tablespoons freshly squeezed lemon juice

1 teaspoon Dijon mustard

1 teaspoon Thai fish sauce

salad

2 large romaine hearts

1 cup freshly grated Parmigiano-Reggiano

2 large green apples, cut into ⅓-inch dice

½ cup chopped pecans, lightly toasted (see sidebar)

❶ In a medium bowl, whisk together the ingredients for the dressing. Set aside.
❷ Wash the romaine and cut the leaves into ¾-inch pieces. Dry well with paper towels and put in a large bowl. Add ½ cup of the cheese and pour in the dressing. Toss gently to coat the leaves and add ¼ cup of the remaining cheese. Toss again. Divide among 6 plates. Sprinkle with a little of the remaining cheese. Garnish each portion with diced apples and toasted pecans.

HOW TO TOAST PECANS

Put the pecans in a small nonstick skillet. Cook over medium-high heat for 2 minutes, stirring constantly, until you smell a faint nutty aroma. Be careful not to burn them! Transfer pecans to a plate and let cool.

PROSCIUTTO "CHOPSTICKS"

If you want to make this salad really special, top it with prosciutto "chopsticks," which are ultra-thin breadsticks, known as grissini, wrapped with a thin slice of prosciutto. Crisscross them on top of the salad. To make them, you need 12 grissini and 12 thin slices prosciutto. Tightly wrap a slice of prosciutto, spiral-fashion, around each breadstick.

SERVE 2 PER PERSON

ENDIVE SALAD WITH FANCY GREENS, WALNUTS AND CRANBERRIES, MAPLE VINAIGRETTE, AND TURKEY "PASTA"

Our tasting panel loved this! The turkey is cut to resemble strands of fettuccine that sit on top of the salad. Belgian endive looks like a pale green torpedo; it is about five inches long and you'll find it in the produce section. Real maple syrup is a must for the addictive dressing. ➪ **SERVES 6**

maple vinaigrette

2 tablespoons real maple syrup

5 tablespoons olive oil

3 tablespoons rice vinegar

2 teaspoons Dijon mustard

1 small garlic clove, pushed through a press or minced

salad

3 large Belgian endives

6 ounces mesclun

½ cup toasted walnut halves (see page 78 for toasting nuts)

½ cup dried cranberries

6 large thin slices of roasted organic turkey breast, about 12 ounces

❶ In a small bowl, whisk together the ingredients for the dressing. Add salt and pepper to taste.

❷ Trim ¼ inch from the bottom of the endives. Laying each endive on its side on a cutting board, cut across the width into ¾-inch pieces. Put in a large bowl with the mesclun. Add the walnuts and cranberries. Toss with the dressing and add a pinch of salt. Divide the salad among 6 large plates.

❸ Cut the turkey into thin strips, about ¼ inch wide, to look like fettuccine. Arrange on top of the salad.

"I love to chop and prepare vegetables with my sharp knives."

DAN

WARM LEMON-CUMIN
CHICKEN ON PITA BREAD SALAD

This is a fantastic dish if you're having friends over for a party. Leftovers make a great lunch for school. Sous-chefs Robyn and Ian Kimmel liked the chicken sliced on top but agreed that it was more fun to eat when the chicken was diced and tossed into the salad. Cumin is a fragrant spice used in many cuisines, including Mexican and Middle Eastern. ⇨ **SERVES 6**

4 large skinless, boneless chicken breasts, about 2 pounds

6 tablespoons olive oil

2 large garlic cloves, pushed through a press or minced

2 tablespoons ground cumin

2 large lemons

3 6-inch pita breads, lightly toasted

1 packed cup finely chopped fresh curly parsley (or cilantro)

½ cup finely chopped scallions

½ cup finely chopped fresh mint

6 large ripe plum tomatoes, finely diced

❶ Put the chicken in a large bowl. Add 2 tablespoons of the oil, the garlic, and 1½ tablespoons cumin. Add the grated zest and juice of 1 lemon. Rub the mixture into the chicken and let sit while you prepare the salad. Preheat the oven to 400 degrees.

❷ Cut the pitas into ¼-inch dice and put in a large bowl. Add the remaining 4 tablespoons of oil and ½ tablespoon of cumin; the parsley, scallions, mint, and tomatoes; and 3 tablespoons of lemon juice from the remaining lemon. Toss well and add salt and pepper.

❸ Put the chicken on a rimmed baking sheet. Sprinkle lightly with salt. Bake for 8 minutes, turn over, and bake for 6 minutes longer or until cooked through. Transfer the chicken to a cutting board. Arrange the salad on a large platter. Cut the warm chicken into thick slices on the bias and place on top of the salad. You can also chop the chicken into small pieces and stir it into the salad.

"I really like using my hands to mix a bowl full of food. It feels like you really get to know the ingredients when you touch them."

ROBYN

TUNA-PASTA NIÇOISE WITH SWEET PEAS

This easy-to-make main-course salad is a blast to eat. It is a combination pasta salad and *salade niçoise* (classically made with tuna, string beans, tomato, and hard-boiled egg) tossed into one! Good for feeding a crowd and especially nice on a picnic. ▷ **SERVES 6**

dressing

3 tablespoons Dijon mustard

1 tablespoon white wine vinegar

1 large garlic clove, pushed through a press or minced

¼ cup olive oil

pasta

6 ounces cellentani or fusilli pasta

5 ounces fresh string beans

1 cup fresh shelled peas

24 grape tomatoes

12 ounces white tuna packed in water

1 tablespoon freshly grated Parmesan

1 lemon

¼ cup chopped fresh chives

2 hard-boiled eggs (see sidebar), cut into wedges

❶ In a small bowl, combine the mustard, vinegar, and garlic. Whisk in the oil until thick and creamy.

❷ Bring a large pot of salted water to a boil. Add the pasta and cook for 5 minutes. Trim the string beans and add to the boiling water. Add the peas. Cook about 7 minutes, until the pasta and vegetables are tender.

❸ Meanwhile, wash the grape tomatoes and cut them in half lengthwise. Place in a large bowl. Drain the tuna and crumble it into the bowl. When the pasta and vegetables are cooked, drain them in a colander under cold water. Pat dry. Add to the bowl with the tuna and tomatoes. Pour the dressing over the mixture. Add the cheese and the juice of 1 lemon. Toss well, adding salt and pepper to taste. Garnish with the chopped chives and wedges of boiled egg.

HOW TO MAKE A PERFECT BOILED EGG

Put eggs in a small saucepan. Cover with cold water and bring to a rapid boil. At this point, cover the pan and remove from the heat. Let sit for 15 minutes. Place the saucepan in the sink and pour off the water. Run cold water over the eggs until they cool. Peel them. They are ready to use, or you may refrigerate them for up to 2 days.

OVERNIGHT VEGETABLE TABBOULEH

This no-cook grain salad, made from bulgur wheat, is an overnight sensation. Assemble it before bedtime and this dish makes itself! I can't resist eating it in the morning, with a hard-boiled egg. For a main-course salad or easy school lunch, add strips of grilled chicken or crumbled feta cheese.

▷ **SERVES 6**

OVER-NIGHT SENSATION

8 ounces dry bulgur wheat, medium grain

3 tablespoons toasted sesame seeds*

½ cup finely chopped carrots, zucchini, or cucumber

½ cup finely chopped red, orange, or yellow bell pepper

2 scallions, finely chopped

½ cup finely chopped green pepper

1 cup tomato juice

⅓ cup freshly squeezed lemon juice

½ cup olive oil

You can buy sesame seeds that are toasted or you can prepare your own: put them in a small nonstick skillet and stir over medium heat until they are golden, about 2 minutes.

Put all the ingredients in a large bowl. Add 1 teaspoon salt and 1 cup cold water. Mix well, cover, and refrigerate overnight. Stir well. Add salt and pepper, if needed, before serving.

STRING BEAN SALAD
WITH FRESH TOMATO CHUTNEY

There are really cool flavors in this simple salad that I re-created from a taste memory of a trip to India. Remember: when dealing with hot peppers you must wash your hands thoroughly with soap and water immediately and not touch your eyes. Peppers contain oils that cause stinging! ▷ **SERVES 6**

2 pounds fresh string beans

1 pint grape tomatoes

1 large garlic clove, peeled

½-inch piece fresh ginger, peeled and chopped

½ small scotch bonnet pepper, seeds removed

1 teaspoon ground cumin

1½ tablespoons dark brown sugar

❶ Trim the ends off the string beans. Bring a large pot of salted water to a boil. Add the string beans and cook for about 6 minutes, until just tender and bright green. Drain in a colander under cold water. Pat dry. Cover and refrigerate until cold.

❷ Wash the tomatoes, dry, and put in the bowl of a food processor. Add the remaining ingredients. Pulse several times until almost smooth. Add salt to taste. Pour the mixture over the string beans and toss. Cover and chill until ready to eat.

SLOPPY SLAW
WITH CARROT-GINGER DRESSING

This dressing uses very little oil and has loads of fresh flavors. It is lovely spooned over sliced cucumbers or poured over chilled, steamed broccoli. I even dip strawberries in it! But we love it best as a cool dressing for slaw. Use either green or savoy cabbage—and shred it as thinly as possible. ▷ **SERVES 6**

carrot-ginger dressing

½ cup diced carrots

1 tablespoon chopped onion

⅓ cup orange juice

2 tablespoons sugar

4 teaspoons rice vinegar

1 teaspoon chopped fresh ginger

1 tablespoon olive oil

slaw

½ large green cabbage

1 cup grated carrots

1 medium red bell pepper

¼ cup freshly minced chives

❶ Put all the dressing ingredients plus ½ teaspoon salt in the bowl of a food processor and process until very smooth. Chill.

❷ Place the cabbage cut side down on a cutting board. Using a sharp, long knife, cut the cabbage into ultrathin slices—it will break apart into shreds. Place the shredded cabbage and grated carrots in a large bowl. Cut the bell pepper into very thin strips and add to the bowl. Pour the dressing over the slaw and toss well. Add salt to taste. Scatter the chives on top. Cover and refrigerate for 1 hour before using. Will last up to 2 days in the refrigerator.

CHAPTER 5 | DINNER SPECIALS WITH VEGETABLES

chocolate chili with cauliflower popcorn ▷ 92

spicy thai tofu with cashews, baby spinach, and red peppers ▷ 93

crunchy wasabi-lime salmon with red cabbage
and sugar snaps ▷ 94

a new kind of chicken "parm" with roasted grape tomatoes ▷ 96

juicy chicken with roasted spaghetti squash ▷ 98

orange-molasses sticky pork with blasted string beans ▷ 100

sun-dried tomato and carrot meatloaf
with fabulous creamed spinach ▷ 103

sizzling skirt steaks and lime with basil, asparagus,
and cherry tomatoes ▷ 104

CHOCOLATE CHILI WITH CAULIFLOWER POPCORN

This delicious vegetarian chili is made dark and mysterious with a touch of semisweet chocolate and cinnamon. Chocolate and cinnamon are used together in several Mexican dishes. Small roasted florets of white cauliflower turn a simple idea into something that looks really dramatic. ▷ **SERVES 6**

½ **pound dried black beans**

2 **large garlic cloves**

4 **tablespoons olive oil**

2 **cups finely chopped onions**

1½ **tablespoons chili powder**

1 **tablespoon ground cumin**

1 **tablespoon dried oregano leaves**

28-**ounce can crushed tomatoes**

¼ **teaspoon ground cinnamon**

1½ **ounces semisweet chocolate, chopped**

1 **large cauliflower**

¼ **cup chopped cilantro or parsley**

❶ Put the beans in a pot and cover with water. Bring to a boil and boil for 2 minutes. Drain the beans in a colander.
❷ Peel the garlic and finely chop. Heat 2 tablespoons of the oil in a 4-quart pot. Add the garlic and onions and cook over medium-high heat for 10 minutes until soft. Add the chili powder, cumin, oregano, and 1 teaspoon salt. Cook, stirring, for 2 minutes until fragrant. Stir in the tomatoes, drained beans, cinnamon, and 5 cups water. Bring to a boil. Lower the heat, cover the pot, and simmer for 1½ hours, stirring often. Add the chocolate and stir until melted. Cook, uncovered, for 30 minutes until thick.

❸ About 40 minutes before serving, preheat the oven to 400 degrees. Cut the cauliflower into ½-inch florets. Put in a bowl and toss with the remaining 2 tablespoons of olive oil and salt to taste. Place on a rimmed baking sheet and roast for 35 minutes until golden. Shake the pan often during baking to prevent sticking. Remove from the oven. Ladle chili into bowls and top with "popcorn" and herbs.

SPICY THAI TOFU WITH CASHEWS, BABY SPINACH, AND RED PEPPERS

Tofu is made from soybeans and is a good source of protein. Alone, it can be bland, but it's so versatile when prepared with flavorful ingredients. Tofu comes in many forms and you can find it at most supermarkets and Asian food stores. Here I use firm blocks of tofu to create an Asian-style stir-fry—complete with veggies and nuts, too. You can serve it over lo mein noodles that cook up in three minutes or fragrant basmati rice. ▷ **SERVES 4**

2 large red bell peppers

3 scallions

3 tablespoons olive oil

3 tablespoons finely minced peeled fresh ginger

3 large garlic cloves, finely chopped

1 pound firm tofu, cut into 1-inch cubes

3 tablespoons soy sauce

Juice of 1 lime

1 teaspoon red pepper flakes

5 ounces baby spinach

⅓ cup chopped fresh basil or cilantro

½ cup roasted cashews

❶ Cut the bell peppers in half lengthwise and remove the seeds. Cut across the width into ½-inch-wide pieces. Trim the scallions and slice thinly on the bias. ❷ Heat the oil in a large wok. Add the ginger, garlic, and bell peppers. Cook over high heat for 2 minutes, stirring constantly. Add the scallions and tofu and cook for 2 minutes, stirring often. Add the soy sauce, lime juice, and red pepper flakes and cook over high heat for 1 minute. Add the spinach and cook, stirring, for 30 seconds. Stir in the basil or cilantro. Add the cashews and cook for 1 minute longer. Adjust the seasonings, adding salt, soy, or more lime juice to taste.

CRUNCHY WASABI-LIME SALMON WITH RED CABBAGE AND SUGAR SNAPS

Here, wasabi-coated peas—a great snack food available in most supermarkets and Asian food stores—get crushed to smithereens to form a crunchy topping whose spiciness lessens as it cooks. The simple stir-fry of red cabbage and sugar snap peas is both beautiful and delicious. Serve with a bowl of steaming jasmine rice. ▷ **SERVES 4**

¾ **cup wasabi peas, about 3 ounces**

4 **6-ounce thick salmon fillets**

1 **large lime**

2 **tablespoons olive oil**

2 **cups sugar snap peas, about 6 ounces**

3½ **cups finely shredded red cabbage, about 10 ounces**

❶ Preheat the oven to 400 degrees. Put the wasabi peas in the bowl of a food processor and process until powdery, but still with tiny pieces.

❷ Sprinkle the fish with salt. Pat the crushed peas onto the fish, making sure that the top is evenly coated. Grate the zest of the lime and sprinkle the zest on top of the fish. Drizzle with 1 tablespoon of the oil. Place the fish on a rimmed baking sheet. Bake for 10 to 12 minutes, until the fish is cooked through.

❸ Meanwhile, trim the ends of the sugar snap peas. Heat the remaining tablespoon of oil in a wok or large nonstick skillet. Add the red cabbage and sugar snaps. Cook over high heat, stirring constantly, for 5 minutes, or until the vegetables are crisp-tender. Add salt to taste. Remove the fish from the oven. Cut the lime in half and squeeze a little lime juice over the fish. Transfer the vegetables to 4 large plates or a platter. Place the fish on the vegetables and serve immediately.

BEAUTIFUL AND DELICIOUS

A NEW KIND OF CHICKEN "PARM" WITH ROASTED GRAPE TOMATOES

Our incredibly juicy rendition of chicken parmigiana goes like this: The chicken is "breaded" with Parmesan cheese, preferably Parmigiano-Reggiano from Italy, topped with roasted grape tomatoes, and covered with mozzarella cheese. It all goes into one pan and is popped into the oven. ▷ **SERVES 6**

¼ cup olive oil

1 large garlic clove

12 ounces grape tomatoes

1½ teaspoons dried oregano leaves

Large pinch of red pepper flakes

6 6-ounce skinless, boneless
   chicken breasts

1¼ cups grated Parmigiano-Reggiano

5 ounces fresh mozzarella,
   thinly sliced

❶ Preheat the oven to 500 degrees.

❷ Put the olive oil in a small bowl. Push the garlic through a press and add to the oil with ½ teaspoon salt. Put the tomatoes in another bowl. Add 2 tablespoons of the "garlic oil," the oregano, and the red pepper flakes. Stir.

❸ Coat the chicken on all sides with the remaining "garlic oil." Put 1 cup of the cheese on a large plate. Dip one side of each chicken breast in the cheese to coat completely. Place the chicken, cheese side up, on one half of a rimmed baking sheet. Place the tomatoes on the other half of the sheet. Bake for 10 minutes, or until the chicken is just firm to the touch.

❹ Place overlapping slices of mozzarella on top of the chicken and pop back into the oven until melted. (Or put it under the broiler for 30 seconds.) Transfer the chicken to plates. Top with the tomatoes and sprinkle with the remaining ¼ cup of cheese.

"I never thought of myself as a great cook, but following these recipes turned me into one."

IAN

JUICY CHICKEN WITH ROASTED SPAGHETTI SQUASH

An original dish by my daughter, Shayna, that truly lives up to its name: a juicy medley of chicken and peppers served on a pile of spaghetti squash "strings." You will need two 9- or 10-inch nonstick skillets to make this dish and a pretty platter to serve it on. Cooking it in two pans maximizes the juiciness of both the vegetables and the chicken. ▷ **SERVES 4**

1 medium spaghetti squash

1 large yellow bell pepper

1 large orange bell pepper

5 ripe plum tomatoes, about 12 ounces

3 tablespoons olive oil

4 large skinless, boneless chicken breasts, 2 pounds

½ cup freshly grated Parmesan

⅓ cup chopped fresh mixed herbs, such as basil, mint, and parsley

❶ Preheat the oven to 400 degrees. Cut the squash in half, lengthwise, and remove the seeds. Place on a baking sheet, cut side down, and bake for 45 minutes, or until soft.

❷ Cut the tops off the bell peppers and then cut the peppers in half. Remove the seeds. Cut into ¼-inch pieces. You will have about 1 cup of each color. Trim the ends of the tomatoes. Coarsely chop so that they are the same size as the bell peppers.

❸ Heat 1½ tablespoons of the oil in a 9- or 10-inch nonstick skillet over medium heat. Add the vegetables and increase the heat to high. Cook for 10 minutes, stirring often, until soft.

❹ Cut the chicken into 1-inch pieces. Heat the remaining 1½ tablespoons of oil in another 9- or 10-inch nonstick skillet. Add the chicken and cook for 3 minutes on one side, or until the pieces become opaque (white), then turn them over and cook for 3 minutes longer, or until just cooked through.

❺ Add the chicken to the vegetables and cook for 1 minute. Transfer the chicken and vegetables to a platter and sprinkle with the cheese.

❻ Using a fork, scrape the spaghetti squash to get "strings." Serve on top of or alongside the chicken. Since not everyone likes the same amount of herbs, Shayna suggests serving them on the side.

ORANGE-MOLASSES STICKY PORK WITH BLASTED STRING BEANS

Here, a zesty ginger-infused marinade does double-duty: it glazes moist pork and makes a thick, sticky sauce for roasted string beans. ▷ **SERVES 4**

½ cup freshly squeezed orange juice

2 tablespoons rice vinegar

1 teaspoon ground cumin

1 tablespoon finely minced peeled fresh ginger

⅓ cup molasses

1 large garlic clove

4 5-ounce center-cut pork chops, boneless

12 ounces string beans

1 small yellow bell pepper

1½ tablespoons olive oil

❶ In a large bowl, whisk together the first five ingredients. Add garlic, pushed through a press. Submerge the pork chops in the marinade. Cover and refrigerate for 2 to 4 hours.

❷ Preheat the oven to 450 degrees. Trim the string beans and put on a rimmed baking sheet. Cut the bell pepper in half, remove the seeds, and cut the pepper into thin strips. Add to the beans. Drizzle 1 tablespoon of the oil over the vegetables and toss. Sprinkle with salt. Roast for 15 minutes, or until browned in spots.

❸ Heat the remaining ½ tablespoon of oil in a large nonstick skillet. Remove the pork from the marinade and put in the hot skillet. Cook over medium-high heat for 5 minutes on each side until golden brown. Sprinkle lightly with salt. Remove the pork from the pan and quickly pour the marinade into the pan and bring it to a boil. Boil for 2 minutes, or until reduced and thickened.

❹ Remove the vegetables from the oven and distribute evenly on 4 plates. Place a pork chop on top and drizzle with marinade.

"I like to feed my family what I cook."

DAN

SUN-DRIED TOMATO AND CARROT MEATLOAF WITH FABULOUS CREAMED SPINACH

The secret to this very juicy meatloaf is the ice-cold water that gets added to the mixture before baking. It has no bread crumbs or filler, just lots of fleshy sun-dried tomatoes and grated carrots. It sits on a bed of the most delicious creamed spinach that can be made in less than 10 minutes! ▷ **SERVES 4**

1 cup sun-dried tomatoes in oil

1 large yellow onion

1½ pounds ground sirloin

½ cup grated carrots

¼ cup finely chopped fresh chives

**Fabulous Creamed Spinach
(see page 114)**

❶ Preheat the oven to 350 degrees.
❷ Drain 2 tablespoons oil from the tomatoes and put it in a nonstick skillet. Finely dice the sun-dried tomatoes. Peel the onion and finely chop. Heat the oil in the skillet and add the onions. Cook over medium-high heat for 10 minutes until very soft, stirring often.
❸ Put the ground beef in a large bowl. Add the diced sun-dried tomatoes, cooked onions and any juices, carrots, chives, 1 teaspoon salt, and ⅓ cup ice-cold water. Mix thoroughly.
❹ Place in a rimmed baking sheet and form into a heart shape or into an 8 x 14½-inch loaf. Bake for 35 to 40 minutes, or until browned and firm to the touch. Let rest 5 minutes and serve with hot creamed spinach.

SIZZLING SKIRT STEAKS AND LIME WITH BASIL, ASPARAGUS, AND CHERRY TOMATOES

Here's a very healthy way to eat a steak, complete with vegetables and full of exciting flavors—including lime, garlic, cumin, and basil. It's great made with chicken breasts, too. ▷ **SERVES 4**

2 skirt steaks, about 1½ pounds

1 tablespoon ground cumin

1 large onion

4 large garlic cloves

2 limes

1 tablespoon sriracha hot sauce

2 tablespoons olive oil

8 thin asparagus spears, cut on the bias

12 cherry tomatoes, cut in half through the stem end

⅓ cup fresh basil leaves, finely julienned

❶ Cut each steak in half so you have 4 equal pieces. Rub with the cumin and season with salt and pepper. Place in a shallow casserole. Peel the onion and cut in half, lengthwise. Place cut side down on a cutting board and slice into thin half-rings. Push the garlic through a press and rub it into the steaks. Toss the steaks with the onion, the zest and juice of 1 lime, and the sriracha sauce. Let sit for 10 minutes.

❷ Heat the oil in a large nonstick skillet until hot. Add the steaks with the onions and the asparagus and sear over high heat for 3 to 4 minutes on each side. Add the tomatoes and basil and cook over high heat for several minutes, until the tomatoes soften. Cut the remaining lime in half and squeeze its juice into the pan. Cook for 1 minute longer, or until the steaks reach the desired doneness. Transfer to a cutting board and cut the steaks on the bias (on a slant) into ½-inch-thick slices. Serve with the vegetables alongside or on top.

EXCITING FLAVORS

CHAPTER

6 ➡️ SIDE DISHES

steaming & roasting ➪ 108

steamed broccoli with cauliflower-cheddar sauce ➪ 109

roasted asparagus with lemon drops ➪ 110
SIDEBAR: TOPPINGS FOR ASPARAGUS 110

roasted root vegetables with maple crumbs ➪ 111

hot and crusty stuffed tomatoes ➪ 112

"looks like mashed potatoes" ➪ 113

fabulous creamed spinach ➪ 114

orange-ginger sweet potato puree ➪ 115

silver-dollar potato pancakes ➪ 116
SIDEBARS: APPLE-CRANBERRY SAUCE, FRESH RHUBARB SAUCE 117

whole-wheat couscous with sweet peas and lemon ➪ 118

ginger-scallion brown rice with carrot nibs ➪ 119

STEAMING & ROASTING

A WORD ABOUT ▷ STEAMING VEGETABLES

For very little money, you can buy a metal steamer basket that has tiny holes in it and metal "petals" that fold up like a flower. It fits neatly into almost any size pot. There are also Chinese bamboo steamers that are flat and also fit inside or on top of a pot of water. The idea is to set the steamer above a few inches of water, which you then bring to a boil. Mound your "prepped" veggies (trimmed and cut into smaller pieces) in the steamer and place the cover on the pot. Cook for 10 to 15 minutes, until the vegetables are just tender. The steam (it's hot!) will cook the vegetables and help retain the nutrients better than boiling will. The vegetables stay bright and true to their color—even better! Green is greener, orange is orangier. Parsnips (my favorite!) taste like candy when steamed. Steamed vegetables are so full of their inherent flavor that they need very little adornment: a drizzle of olive oil, a dollop of sweet butter (page 21), a squeeze of lemon, or a sprinkling of salt.

A WORD ABOUT ▷ ROASTING VEGETABLES

In the early 1990s, restaurant chefs started roasting their vegetables. That means putting them in a very hot oven (400 to 500 degrees) for 15 minutes or so, until the natural sugars begin to caramelize and the vegetables soften and get browned in patches. The vegetables need just a slick of olive oil before they roast into intense flavors on a rimmed baking sheet. Do not put them in a deeper casserole or they will steam. This is a delicious, simple way to cook vegetables, and you can make them easily *in* the oven while you prepare other dishes *on top* of the stove. Asparagus, string beans, cauliflower, Brussels sprouts, sweet potatoes, and broccoli all taste fabulous when prepared this way.

STEAMED BROCCOLI WITH CAULIFLOWER-CHEDDAR SAUCE

Everyone loves broccoli with gobs of cheese sauce. But here's a healthier way: instead of lots of fattening stuff to make the sauce, I puree cooked cauliflower and add some sharp cheddar and Parmesan cheeses. Not only is it delicious, but you get twice as many vegetables and much less fat. It's fun to brag about how you made it. ▷ **SERVES 6**

½ **small cauliflower, about 10 ounces**

1½ **cups milk**

3 **large garlic cloves**

2 **tablespoons grated Parmesan**

4 **ounces very sharp cheddar cheese, shredded**

Cayenne pepper

2 **medium heads of broccoli**

❶ Cut the cauliflower into 1-inch pieces. Put in a small saucepan and add the milk (the milk might not cover the cauliflower). Peel the garlic and cut in half lengthwise. Add to the saucepan and bring to a boil. Cover the pan and cook over medium heat for 15 minutes, or until the cauliflower is very soft.

❷ Transfer the contents of the saucepan to the bowl of a food processor. Process until smooth. Add the Parmesan and all but ⅓ cup of the cheddar cheese. Process until *very* smooth. Transfer the sauce back to the saucepan. Add salt and cayenne to taste.

❸ Meanwhile, bring a large pot of water, fitted with a steamer basket, to a boil. Discard the bottom 2 inches of broccoli stems. Cut the broccoli into long spears. Place in the steamer basket and cover. Cook for 10 minutes, or until the broccoli is tender but still bright green. Reheat the cheese sauce. Transfer the broccoli to a platter. Cover with the cheese sauce and sprinkle with the remaining ⅓ cup of cheese.

ROASTED ASPARAGUS WITH LEMON DROPS

This is the greatest way to make asparagus, especially those nice medium-thick ones you find at the farmers' markets in springtime. Roasting them, instead of poaching them, eliminates that "grassy taste." Just add a gloss of oil with a pastry brush or your fingers and blast them in the oven at high heat for 15 minutes.

▷ **SERVES 4**

1½ pounds medium asparagus

1 tablespoon olive oil

1 small garlic clove

1 lemon

❶ Preheat the oven to 450 degrees.

❷ Snap off the bottom 2 inches of each asparagus spear and trim the ends with a small knife to make them neat. Put the asparagus on a rimmed baking sheet. Drizzle with the olive oil. Push the garlic through a press and, using your hands, rub the oil and garlic over the asparagus. Sprinkle with salt. Roast for 15 minutes until just tender and browned in spots; shake the pan twice during roasting. Squeeze drops of lemon on the asparagus and sprinkle with salt.

TOPPINGS:

Freshly grated Parmesan

Dab of Pesto Presto (page 38)

Toasted pine nuts (pignoli)

Strips of prosciutto

Slivers of sun-dried tomato

Crushed pistachio nuts

Sesame seeds

Sunny-side-up egg and chopped chives

Capers crisped in hot olive oil

Red pepper flakes

Balsamic-Rosemary Vinaigrette (page 76)

Lemon-Parmesan Vinaigrette (page 76)

"They taste better than fries when they get all nice and crispy!"

SHAYNA

ROASTED **ROOT VEGETABLES**
WITH MAPLE CRUMBS

These yummy vegetables are best served hot but are surprisingly delicious at room temperature drizzled with good olive oil and fresh lemon juice. Don't love turnips? Substitute butternut squash or rutabagas, peeled and cut into 1-inch pieces. Great for a crowd, especially at Thanksgiving! ▷ **SERVES 8**

1 pound carrots

1 pound parsnips

1 pound turnips

1¼ pounds Brussels sprouts

4 tablespoons olive oil

¾ cup panko (Japanese bread crumbs) or plain bread crumbs

1 tablespoon real maple syrup

¼ cup finely chopped parsley

❶ Using a vegetable peeler, peel the carrots, parsnips, and turnips. Cut the carrots and parsnips in half lengthwise and then in half across the width. If the bottom halves are too chunky, cut them in half again lengthwise. Cut the turnips into 1-inch chunks. Trim the bottoms of the Brussels sprouts and cut them in half lengthwise. Place the vegetables on a large rimmed baking sheet and toss with 3 tablespoons of the olive oil. Sprinkle with salt and pepper. Roast for 45 minutes, or until the vegetables are tender, tossing several times during baking.

❷ Put the remaining tablespoon of oil in a large nonstick skillet. Heat over medium-high heat and stir in the panko and a large pinch of salt. Cook for 2 or 3 minutes, stirring constantly, until golden. Add the maple syrup and stir until the crumbs are coated. Transfer the hot vegetables to a large platter. Sprinkle heavily with maple crumbs and scatter parsley on top.

YUMMY

HOT AND CRUSTY STUFFED TOMATOES

These are delicious served hot or at room temperature. They are one of our favorite sidekicks for a steak, a simple piece of grilled fish, a dish of pasta tossed with pesto (see page 38), or the meatloaf (see page 103). ▷ **SERVES 4**

4 ripe medium tomatoes

½ cup sliced almonds

⅓ cup freshly grated Parmesan

⅓ cup panko (Japanese bread crumbs) or plain bread crumbs

2 tablespoons olive oil

1 small garlic clove

¼ cup chopped fresh herbs, such as basil, thyme, flat-leaf parsley, or cilantro

❶ Preheat the oven to 425 degrees.

❷ Cut the stem ends off the tomatoes and scoop out ½ inch of tomato flesh. (The top of a tomato is what chefs call the "stem end.") Place the almonds in a small nonstick skillet and toast over medium heat for 2 minutes, stirring until golden. Let cool for 5 minutes. Place the almonds, cheese, panko, oil, garlic, and herbs in the bowl of a food processor and process until crumbly.

❸ Fill the tomato cavities with almond-cheese mixture, mounding it on top. Place the tomatoes in a pie tin. Pour ¼ cup water into the tin. Bake for 20 to 25 minutes, or until the tomatoes are soft and the stuffing is crusted.

"LOOKS LIKE MASHED POTATOES"

Surprise! What looks like the most luxurious offering of buttery, smooth mashed potatoes is instead a puree of cauliflower bound with a bit of potato and sweet butter. The underlying sweetness comes from garlic that gets boiled with the cauliflower. ▷ **SERVES 6**

1 large head of cauliflower,
    about 1½ pounds trimmed

1 large baking potato

2 large garlic cloves, peeled

4 tablespoons (½ stick) unsalted butter

¼ cup milk

6 tablespoons grated Parmesan

❶ Bring a large pot of salted water to a boil. Cut the cauliflower into 1-inch pieces. Peel the potato and cut into ½-inch pieces. Add the cauliflower, potatoes, and garlic to the water. Continue to boil for 16 to 20 minutes, until the vegetables are soft (but not falling apart).

❷ Drain well in a colander and shake dry. Add the cauliflower, potatoes, and garlic to the bowl of a food processor and process until smooth and creamy. Add the butter, milk, and 4 tablespoons of the cheese. Process until very smooth. Add salt and pepper to taste. Serve immediately, sprinkled with the remaining 2 tablespoons of cheese. Or you may make the mixture ahead of time: spoon it into a shallow casserole and sprinkle with the 2 tablespoons of cheese. Bake at 350 degrees until heated through and run it briefly under the broiler until golden.

FABULOUS CREAMED SPINACH

This bright green, creamy spinach takes less than 10 minutes to make. Fresh spinach gets steamed with onion and garlic, then pureed with—surprise!—cottage cheese for an ultrarich texture. The big pot of spinach will shrink to a small amount but you will still have enough for four generous portions. ⇨ **SERVES 4**

1 small onion

1 large garlic clove

16 ounces fresh spinach leaves, washed, with any thick stems removed

1 cup cottage cheese

1½ tablespoons unsalted butter

2 tablespoons grated Parmesan

Sprinkling of grated nutmeg

❶ In the very large pot you use for pasta, put 1 cup water. Cut the onion into paper-thin slices and add to the pot. Peel the garlic and cut in half lengthwise. Add to the pot and bring the water to a boil. Boil for 2 minutes. Add the spinach and ½ teaspoon salt. Cover the pot tight and cook over high heat for 5 minutes, or until the spinach is wilted and tender but still bright green. Transfer the mixture to a colander and press down hard to release all the liquid.

❷ Put the warm spinach mixture in the bowl of a food processor. Add the cottage cheese and butter and process until *very* smooth (all the white flecks will have disappeared). Add salt and pepper to taste. Sprinkle with the cheese and nutmeg.

ORANGE-GINGER
SWEET POTATO PUREE

This amazingly simple, bright orange puree tastes rich and fattening but . . . it's fat-free! I like to add a pinch of five-spice powder, which is a Chinese mixture of spices including star anise, licorice root, and cloves. I also use five-spice in homemade cherry ices (see page 145). ⇨ **SERVES 6**

2 large oranges

4 large sweet potatoes, about 3 pounds

3-inch piece fresh ginger

¼ teaspoon five-spice powder

❶ Grate the zest of the oranges. Cut the oranges in half and squeeze to get ⅔ cup juice. Set aside.
❷ Scrub the potatoes but do not peel. Place in a large pot with water to cover. Bring to a boil; lower the heat to medium. Cook for 50 minutes, or until

the potatoes are very soft. Drain the potatoes and peel under cold water. Cut the potatoes into large pieces and put in the bowl of a food processor.
❸ Using a small knife, peel the ginger and finely chop enough to get 3 tablespoons. Add the ginger, orange zest, and orange juice to the processor. Process until very smooth. Add five-spice powder and salt to taste. Reheat before serving.

SILVER-DOLLAR POTATO PANCAKES

Also known as latkes, these are a really great side dish and are much healthier than fries. We love to make them for breakfast and lunch, too! Applesauce is the most traditional accompaniment, but in springtime try making a chunky rhubarb sauce (see sidebar). ▷ **SERVES 4**

1 pound russet (baking) potatoes

½ small onion

1 extra-large egg, lightly beaten

2 tablespoons whole-wheat flour

1 teaspoon baking powder

¼ cup olive oil

❶ Peel the potatoes and shred them on the large holes of a box grater. Put them in a large bowl. Grate the onion on the large holes of a box grater to get 1 tablespoon onion pulp. Stir it into the potatoes. Using your hands, squeeze the potatoes as hard as you can, over the sink, to get rid of as much liquid as possible. Put the potatoes back into the bowl and add the beaten egg, flour, baking powder, and ½ teaspoon salt.
❷ Heat the oil in a very large nonstick skillet until hot. Carefully place 8 mounds of potato mixture (about 2 tablespoons for each pancake) into the skillet, flattening the mounds with a spatula. Cook for 3 to 4 minutes on one side, turn them over with a spatula, and cook for 2 to 3 minutes on the other side until crispy. Drain on paper towels. Eat them right away or put them on a wire rack placed over a rimmed baking sheet and keep them warm in a 200-degree oven. Do not cover them. Serve with the sauces on the next page.

APPLE-CRANBERRY SAUCE

This simple, delicious applesauce will keep up to one week in the refrigerator—if no one eats it first! You may substitute ground cinnamon or ginger for the allspice.

4 large Granny Smith or a variety of apples, about 1½ pounds

⅔ cup fresh cranberries

⅓ cup turbinado sugar

¼ teaspoon ground allspice

Peel the apples and cut them in half; remove the seeds. Cut into ½-inch pieces. Put the apples, cranberries, sugar, and allspice in a large saucepan. Add 1 cup water. Bring to a boil, lower the heat to a simmer, and cover the pot. Cook for 20 minutes, stirring often. Mash with a potato masher to make a rather smooth sauce (some lumps are fine). Let cool. Cover and refrigerate until cold.

SERVES 4

FRESH RHUBARB SAUCE

If it's springtime, and you're feeling adventurous, try making fresh rhubarb sauce instead of applesauce to serve with your potato pancakes. Botanically speaking, rhubarb is more a vegetable (it is an aquatic grass) than a fruit. It is related to buckwheat but looks like pink celery. It is really tart and needs quite a bit of sugar to balance the taste. Rhubarb springs up in farmers' markets—and supermarkets—in April. Be sure to remove any dark green leaves; they are poisonous.

1 pound fresh rhubarb

½ fresh vanilla bean*

½ cup turbinado sugar

Trim the rhubarb and cut it into 1-inch pieces. Put in a large saucepan. Cut the vanilla bean in half, lengthwise, and using the tip of a small sharp knife, remove the little vanilla seeds from the bean, scraping inside the small channel. Don't lose the seeds! Add them to the saucepan with the sugar and ⅓ cup water. Bring to a boil; lower the heat to medium and cook, stirring often, until the rhubarb has broken down into a sauce that looks like chunky applesauce, about 12 to 15 minutes. Add a pinch of salt. Remove from the heat. Serve warm or at room temperature.

SERVES 4

*You may stick the scraped vanilla bean in a jar of granulated sugar to flavor the sugar. It lasts indefinitely. Use the vanilla sugar for baking and to sweeten drinks.

WHOLE-WHEAT COUSCOUS WITH SWEET PEAS AND LEMON

Couscous is a form of pasta that is rolled into teeny balls. It is most often used in dishes from North Africa, Israel, Sicily, and the south of France; it is now easy to find in America. The secret here is to fluff up the couscous after its brief steam bath. Great with grilled fish or chicken or all by itself. ▷ **SERVES 4**

1 lemon

1½ cups chicken or vegetable broth

1 cup small fresh green peas*

1 cup whole-wheat couscous

1½ tablespoons olive oil

2 tablespoons grated Parmesan

Minced fresh chives

❶ Grate the zest of the lemon. Cut the lemon in half and squeeze to get 2 tablespoons juice. Set aside.

❷ Put the broth in a medium saucepan with a cover. Add ¼ cup water and bring to a boil. Add the peas and cook for about 10 minutes, until they are tender but still bright green. Add the couscous and cook for 30 seconds, stirring constantly. Add the lemon zest, lemon juice, and olive oil, and stir.

❸ Cover the pot and remove it from the heat. Let sit for 5 minutes. Remove the cover and fluff the couscous with a fork to separate the grains. Add salt and pepper to taste. Sprinkle with the cheese and chives and serve.

If fresh peas are not available, use frozen peas but cook them for only 2 minutes once they're added to the broth.

"It's so much more satisfying to eat it and know you made it."

ROSIE

GINGER-SCALLION BROWN RICE WITH CARROT NIBS

Good health includes eating whole grains and brown rice. But no one makes them this way—studded with fresh ginger, golden raisins, and fresh carrots chopped up to form "nibs." ⇨ **SERVES 8**

2 large carrots

1½ cups brown rice

1 large bunch of scallions

2 tablespoons unsalted butter

2 tablespoons finely minced peeled fresh ginger

⅔ cup golden raisins

❶ Peel the carrots and cut them into 1-inch pieces. Put them in the bowl of a food processor and pulse 8 to 10 times until they are finely chopped.

❷ In a 2-quart saucepan put 3½ cups water and 1 teaspoon salt. Bring to a boil, add the rice, stir, and reduce the heat to low. Cover the pot and cook for 20 minutes, stirring once. Add the carrots and cook for 10 minutes.

❸ Meanwhile, remove the roots from the scallions. Thinly slice the white and light green parts to get about ⅔ cup. Chop ¼ cup of the dark green part for later. Melt the butter in a large skillet. Add the scallions and ginger and cook over medium heat for 3 minutes, stirring until soft. Set aside.

❹ After 30 minutes, add the raisins and scallion mixture to the rice. Cook for 2 minutes longer. Remove from the heat; fluff the rice with a fork. Add salt and pepper to taste. Scatter chopped dark greens on top.

CHAPTER 7 DESSERTS & DRINKS

danielle's fresh apple crisp ▷ 123

tower of peaches ▷ 125

roasted pears with toasted almonds, maple drizzle ▷ 127

freshest fruit salad with cinnamon-sugar wontons ▷ 128
SIDEBAR: HOW TO CUT A PINEAPPLE 129

hot-milk shortcakes with strawberries and "cream" ▷ 131

chocolate mousse cake with raspberries ▷ 132

rosemary-lemon custard cakes ▷ 135

shayna's healthy birthday cake ▷ 136

very moist zucchini-banana cake ▷ 138

olive oil–chocolate chip cookies ▷ 140

buttermilk ice cream ▷ 142

honeydew-kiwi sorbet ▷ 144

fresh and spicy cherry ices ▷ 145

watermelon lemonade ▷ 146

irene's agua fresca ▷ 147

cantaloupe sherbet ▷ 148
SIDEBAR: FRESH STRAWBERRY SAUCE 148

fresh strawberry breeze ▷ 148

maple snow ▷ 149

mulled red cider ▷ 149

iced green-lemongrass tea ▷ 150

hot strawberry tea ▷ 151

"I made up this recipe using granola because I really like snacking on it. It is very natural, but also sweet and crunchy. I thought it would make a nice topping for the soft-cooked apples. After apple picking in the fall, when you have a nice mixture of fresh apples, this is a fun recipe to make."

DANIELLE

EAT FRESH FOOD

DANIELLE'S FRESH APPLE CRISP

This is Danielle Hartog's wonderful recipe for autumn—when a wide variety of snappy, crisp apples is available at your farmers' market or a local orchard. Use many different kinds to get the most complex and luscious flavor. ⇨ **SERVES 8**

4 tablespoons (½ stick) unsalted butter

½ cup real maple syrup

1 tablespoon whole-wheat flour

1½ teaspoons ground cinnamon

2 tablespoons freshly squeezed orange juice

8 assorted large apples, peeled, cored, and sliced

3 cups granola

❶ Preheat the oven to 350 degrees.

❷ Using 1 tablespoon of the butter, grease an 8-cup soufflé dish or a 9 x 13-inch casserole.

❸ In a large bowl, stir together the maple syrup, flour, cinnamon, and orange juice. Add the apples and stir to coat. Place the mixture in the soufflé dish or casserole. Bake for 25 minutes.

❹ Put the granola and the remaining 3 tablespoons of butter in the bowl of a food processor. Process until moist crumbs form. Sprinkle the granola mixture on top of the apples, pressing down lightly, and bake for 20 minutes longer, until golden and bubbly. Serve warm or at room temperature.

EAT FRESH FOOD

TOWER OF PEACHES

Here, stacks of crispy honey-glazed wontons become a tower of goodness when layered with fresh fruit. Peaches, nectarines, and plums are known as stone fruit because their large pits resemble stones. They can be used alone or together in this gorgeous summer dessert. ➯ **SERVES 4**

16 square wonton wrappers

⅔ cup honey

6 large ripe peaches

Fresh mint, tarragon, or lavender

❶ Preheat the oven to 375 degrees. Place the wontons on a rimmed baking sheet. Heat ⅓ cup of the honey in a small saucepan. Using a pastry brush, spread the honey lightly on each wonton to cover completely. Bake for 6 to 8 minutes until golden and crisp.

❷ Wash the fruit and dry well. Cut in half and remove the pits. Cut each half into thin wedges and place in a medium bowl. Pour the remaining ⅓ cup of honey over peaches and stir.

❸ Place 1 wonton in the center of each of 4 plates. Top the wonton with some of the fruit. Place another flat wonton on top. Make two more layers of fruit and wontons. Top with a wonton and the remaining fruit. Garnish with mint, tarragon, or lavender.

ROASTED PEARS WITH TOASTED ALMONDS, MAPLE DRIZZLE

Roasting pears concentrates their wonderful flavor and softens them at the same time (but doesn't make them mushy like canned pears). Any ripe variety of pear will do: I especially love Comice and Bartlett. Real maple syrup (not imitation or pancake syrup) is a must. ▷ **SERVES 4**

2 very large just-ripe pears

2 cinnamon sticks

1 lime

⅓ cup real maple syrup

½ cup thick Greek yogurt

¼ cup sliced almonds, lightly toasted (see page 78)

❶ Preheat the oven to 400 degrees.

❷ Peel the pears using a vegetable peeler. Cut in half lengthwise and, using a melon baller, remove the core and seeds. Place cut side down in a pie tin. Snap the cinnamon sticks in half and place in the dish. Cut the lime in half and squeeze its juice over the pears. Pour the maple syrup on top. Bake for 30 to 35 minutes, or until tender when pierced with a knife, turning the pears over after 20 minutes. Baste with the juices in the baking dish.

❸ Remove the pears and place them in a large shallow bowl. Put the pan juices in a small saucepan and boil over high heat for 1 minute. Pour over the pears. Dollop with the yogurt and scatter the almonds on top.

FRESHEST FRUIT SALAD
WITH CINNAMON-SUGAR WONTONS

Sous-chef Evan Chender brings all the elements of these fruits together with a simple syrup, made with honey instead of sugar and flecked with vanilla seeds. In season, he suggests we add our own favorite fruits at their peak of flavor. I like to serve them with my cinnamon-sugar cookies—made from wonton skins! They take less than ten minutes to make. ▷ **SERVES 8**

⅓ cup honey

1 vanilla bean

1 ripe pineapple

1 ripe cantaloupe

2 pints ripe strawberries

3 ripe kiwi

Small bunch of fresh mint

❶ Put the honey and 1 cup water in a saucepan. Open the vanilla bean by carefully cutting it in half, lengthwise. Use the tip of a small knife to scrape the seeds into the saucepan. Reserve the bean to make vanilla sugar (see note, page 117). Bring to a boil and boil for 2 minutes. Let cool.

❷ Peel the pineapple with a sharp knife. Cut in half lengthwise and remove the core. Cut the pineapple into ½-inch pieces and then put them into a large bowl. Cut the cantaloupe in half and remove the seeds. Cut away the rind and cut the flesh into ½-inch pieces or simply scoop out the flesh using a melon baller. Add to the bowl.

❸ Wash the strawberries and remove the stems. Cut in half lengthwise and add to the bowl. Peel the kiwi and cut into ¼-inch slices (cut across the width) or into ½-inch pieces. Add to the bowl. Pour the honey syrup over the fruit, cover, and chill until ready to serve. Garnish with mint.

SPRING
Mangoes, apricots, poached rhubarb

SUMMER
Blueberries, peaches, nectarines, sweet cherries, blackberries, black raspberries, watermelon

FALL
Diced pears, plums, fresh figs, grapes

WINTER
Grapefruit, tangerines, oranges, lady apples, bananas

TO MAKE
CINNAMON-SUGAR

Mix ½ cup granulated sugar with
1 teaspoon ground cinnamon.

MAKES ½ CUP

CINNAMON-SUGAR
WONTONS

16 wonton wrappers

1 tablespoon melted butter or olive oil

3 tablespoons cinnamon-sugar

Preheat the oven to 400 degrees.
Place the wontons on a rimmed
baking sheet. Using a pastry brush,
brush the wontons evenly with the
melted butter or oil. Sprinkle evenly
with the cinnamon-sugar. Bake for 6 to
8 minutes, or until just crisp. Let cool on
pan. Remove with spatula.

MAKES 16

HOW TO CUT
A PINEAPPLE

Select a ripe, fragrant pineapple.
You can tell by smelling it and by
pulling a leaf out of the crown. If it pulls
out easily, the pineapple is ripe. Cut
off the top and then cut lengthwise
into 4 large wedges. Make lengthwise
cuts to remove the core, and discard.
Cut the flesh into pieces.

HOT-MILK SHORTCAKES
WITH STRAWBERRIES AND "CREAM"

Baked in custard cups, these tender vanilla cakes are layered with strawberries and topped with billows of thick, lightly sweetened yogurt. If you can find it, use Greek yogurt, which is thick and creamy. ⟹ **SERVES 6**

2 extra-large eggs

½ cup plus 3 tablespoons sugar

¾ teaspoon pure vanilla extract

1¼ cups self-rising flour

⅔ cup milk

3½ tablespoons unsalted butter

16 ounces large ripe strawberries

1½ cups plain Greek yogurt

¼ cup confectioners' sugar

❶ Preheat the oven to 425 degrees.

❷ In the bowl of an electric mixer, beat the eggs on high speed until thick, about 3 minutes. Add ½ cup of the sugar and beat 1 minute longer. Add ½ teaspoon of the vanilla extract and the flour and beat for 30 seconds.

❸ Put the milk and butter in a small saucepan and bring just to a boil, stirring until the butter melts. Add to the batter and beat for 30 seconds.

❹ Spray 6 custard cups with cooking spray. Pour the batter into the cups and place the cups on a baking sheet. Bake for 16 minutes, until firm and golden. Remove from the oven and let cool.

❺ Meanwhile, wash the berries and remove the stems. Cut lengthwise into 3 or 4 thin slices. Put in a bowl with the remaining 3 tablespoons of sugar and toss. In another bowl, stir together the yogurt, confectioners' sugar, and the remaining ¼ teaspoon of vanilla until smooth.

❻ Remove the cakes from the cups. Cut a ½-inch slice from the top of each cake. Cover with a portion of berries and top with a "hat." Spoon the sweetened yogurt on top and garnish with more berries.

CHOCOLATE MOUSSE CAKE WITH RASPBERRIES

You will feel like a four-star chef when you make this flourless cake. It is rich and chocolaty with a soft, oozing center. Be careful not to overbake. Delicious served slightly warm. ▷ **SERVES 10**

4 extra-large eggs

Zest of 1 small orange

6 tablespoons (¾ stick) unsalted butter

1 tablespoon olive oil, plus more for greasing the pan

12 ounces semisweet chocolate

1 pint fresh raspberries

2 tablespoons confectioners' sugar

❶ Preheat the oven to 350 degrees.

❷ Put the eggs and a pinch of salt in the bowl of an electric mixer or use a hand-held electric mixer. It is important to use a mixer because the eggs need to triple in volume and get very thick. Beat the eggs on high speed for 5 minutes. Stir in the orange zest.

❸ Meanwhile, put the butter, olive oil, and chocolate in a heavy medium saucepan. Stir over low heat for several minutes, until the chocolate melts and the mixture is smooth.

❹ Using a flexible rubber spatula, add the chocolate mixture to the beaten eggs and beat on low speed until the batter is completely smooth. Using a little additional olive oil, coat the inside of an 8½-inch cake pan. Cut out a round of parchment paper or foil to fit in the bottom of the pan. Pour in the batter. Bake for 18 to 20 minutes; the center should still be very soft. Remove from the oven.

❺ Wash the berries and dry well. Put the berries side by side on top of the cake to cover completely. Dust with the confectioners' sugar right before serving. The best way to do this is to push the sugar through a fine-mesh strainer. Serve slightly warm.

MAGICAL

134   EAT FRESH FOOD

ROSEMARY-LEMON CUSTARD CAKES

These magical little confections separate into custard with a layer of cake floating on top. The flavors of lemon and rosemary make more magic in your mouth. ▷ **SERVES 6**

3 extra-large eggs

¼ cup plus ⅓ cup sugar

2 large lemons

2 tablespoons unsalted butter, at room temperature

¼ cup unbleached white flour

1 teaspoon finely minced fresh rosemary

1½ cups milk

1 tablespoon confectioners' sugar

❶ Preheat the oven to 350 degrees.

❷ Separate the whites and yolks of the eggs. Beat the egg whites and a pinch of salt at medium-high speed in the bowl of an electric mixer until foamy. Slowly add the ¼ cup sugar, 1 tablespoon at a time, beating until stiff peaks form, about 4 minutes.

❸ Grate the zest of both lemons using a Microplane grater or the fine holes of a box grater. Set aside. Cut the lemons in half and squeeze into a small bowl to get ⅓ cup juice.

❹ In a separate bowl, beat together the ⅓ cup sugar and the butter at medium speed of a mixer until creamy, about 2 minutes. Beat in the flour, lemon zest and juice, and rosemary. Add the yolks and milk, and beat well. Use a rubber spatula and gently stir in the egg white

mixture. Spoon equally into six 5-ounce custard cups. Place the cups in a baking dish and add very hot tap water to the dish to a depth of 1 inch.

❺ Carefully put the dish in the oven and bake for 45 minutes, or until the cakes are firm and golden. Using pot holders, remove the dish from oven and remove the cups from the dish. Let cool. Cover and refrigerate until very cold, at least 4 hours. Sprinkle with confectioners' sugar, pushed through a sieve, and eat them from the cups. Or you can unmold from the cups: using a butter knife, loosen the custards around the edge of the cup, then place a small plate on top and turn them upside down. Garnish each with a fresh rosemary sprig.

> *"I loved the Rosemary Custard Cakes so much! There was an extra one and we all fought over it. I will make this all the time. They are amazingly great!"*
> **SOPHIE**

SHAYNA'S HEALTHY BIRTHDAY CAKE

Here's a sweet treat that says "party"—and you can put it together in no time at all. My daughter, Shayna, invented it one afternoon, with no recipe to use as a guideline. Her goal was to make a healthful birthday cake (using olive oil instead of butter). Here's the result, studded with super-fresh fragrant strawberries and diced bananas. For ultimate pleasure, you gotta have milk. Serve the cake slightly warm and the milk very cold. Use the organic, all-natural sprinkles that are now available in many supermarkets. Make a wish! ▷ **SERVES 10**

3 extra-large eggs

⅓ cup olive oil

1 teaspoon pure vanilla extract

¾ cup unbleached white flour

¾ cup self-rising flour

6 tablespoons sugar

1 cup diced bananas

1 cup diced strawberries

¾ cup miniature chocolate chips

**3 tablespoons organic
    confetti sprinkles**

❶ Preheat the oven to 375 degrees.

❷ Crack the eggs into a medium bowl.
Using a wire whisk, beat the eggs well.

Whisk in the olive oil, vanilla, and ¼ cup
water. Beat well. In a larger bowl, stir
together the flours and 5 tablespoons
sugar. Whisk this into the egg mixture
and beat until it is smooth and creamy
(no lumps).

❸ Lightly oil an 8-inch cake pan. Pour
half of the batter into the pan. Sprinkle
evenly with the bananas and strawberries. Sprinkle 1 tablespoon sugar on
top. Scatter ½ cup of the chocolate
chips over all. Top with the remaining
batter. Sprinkle with the remaining ¼
cup of chips and scatter sprinkles on
top. Bake for 35 minutes, until just firm
and golden. Let cool on a wire rack.

VERY MOIST
ZUCCHINI-BANANA CAKE

You will love this cake, also called tea bread, as its mysterious flavor and moisture comes from a ripe banana and a zucchini! Nice with a scoop of homemade Buttermilk Ice Cream (page 142). ⇨ **SERVES 8**

1 large zucchini, about 10 ounces

2 extra-large eggs

¾ cup turbinado sugar

⅔ cup olive oil, plus more for greasing the pan

2 teaspoons pure vanilla extract

2 teaspoons ground cinnamon

1 very ripe medium banana

½ cup golden raisins

1½ cups self-rising flour

❶ Preheat the oven to 350 degrees.
❷ Wash the zucchini and dry; do not peel. Grate the zucchini on the large holes of a box grater to get 2 cups. Using your clean hands, squeeze the zucchini dry.
❸ In the bowl of an electric mixer beat the eggs and sugar on medium-high for 3 minutes. Add the oil, vanilla, and cinnamon and beat for 30 seconds. Peel the banana and break it into small pieces. Add the banana to the bowl.

Beat until the banana is incorporated and the mixture is smooth. Stir in the zucchini and raisins, then slowly add the flour and mix well.
❹ Lightly oil a nonstick 8 x 4-inch loaf pan. Pour in the batter and bake for 45 minutes, until firm and golden. Remove from the oven and let cool. Turn bread out of pan and slice.

OLIVE OIL–CHOCOLATE CHIP **COOKIES**

These cookies look so professional—like those you might buy at an Italian pastry shop. The bonus is that these are much healthier. They are also delicious coated in sesame seeds instead of chocolate. ▷ **MAKES 24**

2 cups self-rising flour

⅔ cup sugar

2 extra-large eggs

½ cup olive oil

1½ teaspoons pure vanilla extract

½ teaspoon pure almond extract

6 ounces miniature chocolate chips

❶ Preheat the oven to 325 degrees.
❷ Put the flour and sugar in the bowl of an electric mixer. In a separate bowl, whisk together the eggs, olive oil, and vanilla and almond extracts. Add the wet mixture to the flour mixture and mix until a smooth dough forms. The mixture will be slightly crumbly and a little oily.

❸ Knead several times on the counter. Form into 24 balls and then shape into small ovals that are 1½ inches long and ¾ inch wide. Roll the tops in miniature chocolate chips. Line a large rimmed baking sheet with parchment paper or use a Silpat pad. Place the cookies 1 inch apart. Bake for 25 minutes, or until firm to the touch. Remove from the oven and let cool on the pan. Remove with a spatula.

BUTTERMILK ICE CREAM

This is sooo good. It tastes like cheesecake yet is extremely low in fat.
Serve with Cinnamon-Sugar Wontons (page 129) or with fresh berries.

▷ **SERVES 6 TO 8**

1¾ cups sugar

½ cup freshly squeezed lemon juice

1 quart (4 cups) buttermilk

1 teaspoon pure vanilla extract

❶ Put the sugar in a large bowl. Add the lemon juice and stir until the sugar dissolves. Stir in buttermilk, vanilla extract, and a pinch of salt.

❷ Cover and chill for several hours. Freeze in an ice-cream maker according to the manufacturer's directions.

"I never thought I could make ice cream better than store-bought!"
STEPH

"Rozanne's recipes rock!"
STEPH & ROSIE

HONEYDEW-KIWI SORBET

Honeydew melons and kiwi fruit are available all year long and can make any day feel like summer. The sorbet is a beautiful jade-green color with black polka dots. Serve it with a wedge of honeydew or in a glass. ▷ **SERVES 6**

½ cup sugar

½ large ripe honeydew melon, about 1½ pounds

4 large ripe kiwi

1 lime

❶ In a small saucepan, bring the sugar and ½ cup water to a boil. Stir until the sugar dissolves and the liquid is clear, about 2 minutes. Set aside.

❷ Scoop out seeds from melon using a large spoon. Scoop out flesh of melon. Peel the kiwi using a small sharp knife. Cut the melon and kiwi into 1-inch pieces and place in the bowl of a food processor. Add a pinch of salt and process until very smooth. Add the sugar syrup and process again until smooth.

❸ Cover and refrigerate until very cold. Freeze in an ice-cream maker according to the manufacturer's directions.

FRESH AND SPICY CHERRY ICES

Yum, this is such a great flavor combo. Five-spice powder is a Chinese spice blend made from star anise, licorice root, clove, fennel, and red pepper. I keep it in my pantry and also use it for sweet potatoes (see page 115). This is best made in summer when fresh cherries are at their juiciest and have the best flavor. ➪ **SERVES 6**

¾ cup turbinado sugar

Zest and juice of 1 lemon

½ teaspoon five-spice powder

1½ pounds ripe red cherries

❶ In a small saucepan, put 2¼ cups water, the sugar, lemon zest and juice (about 2 tablespoons), and five-spice powder. Bring to a boil and boil for 2 minutes, or until the sugar dissolves. Let cool.

❷ To remove the pits from the cherries, either cut the cherries in half and pick out the pits or use a cherry pitter. Discard the pits. Place the pitted cherries in the bowl of a food processor and process until smooth. Slowly add the sugar syrup and process until very smooth. Refrigerate until very cold. Freeze in an ice-cream maker according to the manufacturer's directions.

WATERMELON
LEMONADE

This is our favorite party drink. Double the recipe if you have lots of guests. ⊳ **SERVES 4**

1½ pounds cut-up watermelon

4 large lemons

⅓ cup honey

❶ Remove rind and any seeds from the watermelon. Cut the watermelon into chunks and put in the bowl of a food processor. Process until very smooth. Transfer to a large pitcher.
❷ Using the fine holes of a box grater, or a Microplane grater, grate the zest of 1 lemon. Cut that lemon and 2 more lemons in half and squeeze to get ¾ cup juice. Put the zest and lemon juice in a bowl. Stir the honey into the lemon juice until dissolved. Add this mixture to the watermelon juice. Stir in 1½ cups cold water. Cover and refrigerate until cold. Serve over ice. Garnish with thin lemon slices.

IRENE'S AGUA FRESCA

My friend Irene Hernandez, from Puebla, Mexico, makes this agua fresca—or "fruit water"—for me when she comes to visit. You can make it with cantaloupe, honeydew, papaya, or watermelon. It doesn't require much sugar; just let the fresh fruit flavors shine through. If you add a splash of seltzer, you'll have a delicious fresh fruit "soda." ▷ **SERVES 4**

½ large ripe cantaloupe or honeydew

¼ cup sugar

**Slices of lemon, lime, or extra fruit,
   for garnish**

❶ Remove any seeds and rind from the melon. Cut the fruit into large chunks and put in a blender or in the bowl of a food processor. Add the sugar and 1 cup water. Process on high until very smooth. You will have 3 cups of liquid. Put in a pitcher and add 3 cups cold water. Cover and refrigerate until cold. This will last up to 2 days in the refrigerator. Stir well before serving.
❷ Garnish with a small piece of the fruit you used, and with slices of lemon or lime. Serve over ice, if you wish.

CANTALOUPE SHERBET

Unlike ices or sorbet, sherbet has a bit of dairy in it. Pale orange in color, this version looks beautiful garnished with a handful of fresh blueberries or with my fresh strawberry sauce below. Or you can simply garnish with an unusual variety of mint: I have found "chocolate" mint and "pineapple" mint at my local farmers' market, but you can use spearmint or peppermint, which are more common. I grow them both in my window box. ▷ **SERVES 6**

1 small very ripe cantaloupe

7 tablespoons honey

1 cup milk

1 small bunch of fresh mint, for garnish

❶ Cut the cantaloupe in half and remove the seeds. Cut the flesh into chunks and put in the bowl of a food processor. Process until very smooth. You will have about 2 cups.

❷ Put the honey and milk in a small saucepan. Add a pinch of salt and cook over medium-high heat, stirring constantly, until the honey melts, about 1 minute. Let cool and stir into the cantaloupe puree. Chill until cold and freeze in an ice-cream maker according to the manufacturer's directions. Garnish with the mint, fresh strawberry sauce, or fresh blueberries.

FRESH STRAWBERRY SAUCE

8 ounces very ripe strawberries

2 tablespoons turbinado sugar

Wash the strawberries and pat dry. Remove the green stems. Put the berries in the bowl of a food processor with the sugar. Process until very smooth.

MAKES 1 CUP

FRESH STRAWBERRY BREEZE

Here's a cold drink using fresh apple cider that turns a beautiful shade of pink with a frothy light pink cap. Some of the sous-chefs invented it one very hot day. ▷ **SERVES 2 OR 3**

10 large very ripe strawberries

2½ cups fresh apple cider

Wash the berries and remove the stems. Slice thick; you should have 1 packed cup. Place in a blender with the apple cider. Blend until very smooth and frothy. Pour over ice.

MAPLE SNOW

We love eating this—generally first thing in the morning—after a deep new snowfall when the snow is clean and powdery. We call it Winter Ices. ▷ **SERVES 4**

4 cups freshly fallen snow

⅔ cup pure maple syrup

1 lemon, halved

A handful of diced strawberries

Put the snow in 4 pretty glasses or dessert cups and place in the freezer while you prepare the syrup. Put the syrup in a small saucepan and bring to a boil. Boil 1 minute, or until slightly thickened, and add a pinch of salt. Pour over the snow. Add a squeeze of lemon juice and top with berries.

MULLED RED CIDER

This is especially nice during the holidays and will make your house smell heavenly. It is also delicious iced. ▷ **SERVES 6**

1 quart (4 cups) fresh apple cider

2 cinnamon sticks

1 strip of orange zest

2 rosehip tea bags

❶ Put the apple cider in a large saucepan. Add the cinnamon sticks and orange zest and bring to a boil. Lower the heat and simmer for 10 minutes. Remove from the heat and add the tea bags.

❷ Let steep for 10 minutes. Remove the tea bags and cinnamon sticks. Serve immediately or gently reheat before serving.

ICED GREEN-LEMONGRASS TEA

Green tea is known to be very healthful, full of antioxidants and other good things for your body. Lemongrass, a long pale green stalk, is a staple of Thai cooking and adds a mysterious citrusy flavor. You can find it in the produce section of many supermarkets. ▷ **SERVES 4**

2 stalks lemongrass

2 tablespoons honey

2 tablespoons green tea leaves

1 lime

❶ Tear off the tough outer leaves from the lemongrass stalks and discard. Finely chop the remaining lemongrass stalks, including the darker tops.
❷ In a large saucepan, put 5 cups water, the chopped lemongrass, and the honey. Bring to a rapid boil, lower the heat, and simmer for 10 minutes. Remove from the heat and stir in the tea. Cover the saucepan and let steep for 2 minutes. If you leave it longer, the tea becomes bitter. Strain the tea through a strainer into a pitcher. Discard the contents of the strainer. Refrigerate the tea until very cold. Serve over ice with a wedge of lime.

HOT STRAWBERRY TEA

This is an unusual hot drink, the color of roses. I call it tea but it has no caffeine—just the sweet ripe flavors of strawberry tinged with the scent of lemon and basil.

▷ **SERVES 4**

8 ounces very ripe strawberries

3 tablespoons turbinado sugar

4 large basil leaves

1 lemon

❶ Wash the berries and dry. Remove the stems from the berries.

❷ Place the hulled berries and the sugar in the bowl of a food processor and process until it becomes a smooth puree. Put into a large heat-proof pitcher.

❸ Bring 4 cups water to a boil and pour into the pitcher. Add the basil leaves. Cover and let steep for 15 minutes. Strain through a fine-mesh sieve into 4 warm cups. Cut the lemon in half and squeeze a few drops of lemon juice into the tea. Float a thin slice of lemon on top.

MENUS

When creating delectable menus, the dishes need
to be in harmony with the seasons and they
need to tell a story. With just four or five recipes
you can create a mood, celebrate a holiday, or plan
a party. Good menus have a balance of flavors
and contrasts of textures and temperatures. Follow
the calendar and use ingredients in season.
Here are a dozen ideas. Now it's time to make
your own menu magic.

NEW YEAR'S BREAKFAST

"Pink Flamingo" Yogurt Smoothie
Ultra-Thin Breakfast Crepes with Fresh Blueberry Syrup
Grape-and-Pignoli Breakfast Cake
Mulled Red Cider

WINTER DINNER PARTY

Onion Soup with Apple Cider and Thyme
A Loaf of Whole-Wheat Bread
Orange-Molasses Sticky Pork with Blasted String Beans
"Looks Like Mashed Potatoes"
Rosemary-Lemon Custard Cakes

VALENTINE'S DAY DINNER

Carrot-Ginger-Tomato Soup, Fried Carrot Tops
Eggless Caesar with Toasted Pecans, Green Apple "Croutons"
Sun-Dried Tomato and Carrot Meatloaf with Fabulous Creamed Spinach
Chocolate Mousse Cake with Raspberries
Hot Strawberry Tea

PICNIC IN THE PARK

Juicy Red Gazpacho
Guacamole with Jicama Pick-Up Sticks
Tuna-Pasta Niçoise with Sweet Peas
Overnight Vegetable Tabbouleh
Olive Oil–Chocolate Chip Cookies
Watermelon Lemonade

A BIRTHDAY PARTY

Farmers' Market Pizza, Baking Powder Crust
Bombay Sliders with Hurry-Curry Sauce
Sloppy Slaw with Carrot-Ginger Dressing
Mac-and-Cheese with Cauliflower and Creamy Red Pepper Sauce
Shayna's Healthy Birthday Cake
Irene's Agua Fresca

AN ASIAN LUNCH

Spicy Sesame Noodles with Crunchy Snow Peas
Asian Summer Rolls, Fun Sauce
Honeydew-Kiwi Sorbet
Cinnamon-Sugar Wontons
Iced Green-Lemongrass Tea

ON MOTHER'S DAY

Pasta Primavera with Jade Zucchini Sauce
Crunchy Wasabi-Lime Salmon with Red Cabbage and Sugar Snaps
Roasted Asparagus with Lemon Drops
Whole-Wheat Couscous with Sweet Peas and Lemon
Hot-Milk Shortcakes with Strawberries and "Cream"

FOR FATHER'S DAY

Lemony Whole-Wheat Ziti with Broccoli, Parsnips, and Prosciutto
Sizzling Skirt Steaks and Lime with Basil, Asparagus, and
    Cherry Tomatoes
Fabulous Creamed Spinach
Silver-Dollar Potato Pancakes
Cantaloupe Sherbet with Fresh Strawberry Sauce

WARM-WEATHER LUNCH

Very Fresh Vegetable Soup
Great Fish Tacos
Sloppy Slaw with Carrot-Ginger Dressing
Buttermilk Ice Cream
Fresh Strawberry Breeze

LAST GASP OF SUMMER

"Straw-and-Hay" with Uncooked Tomato Sauce
Warm Lemon-Cumin Chicken on Pita Bread Salad
Freshest Fruit Salad
Fresh and Spicy Cherry Ices

AUTUMN WEEKEND

Risi e Bisi
Endive Salad with Fancy Greens, Walnuts and Cranberries,
    Maple Vinaigrette, and Turkey "Pasta"
Juicy Chicken with Roasted Spaghetti Squash
Danielle's Fresh Apple Crisp

HOLIDAY PARTY

Peanut Butter Hummus with Crudités
BBQ Onion and Smoked Gouda Quesadilla
Chocolate Chili with Cauliflower Popcorn
Very Moist Zucchini-Banana Cake
Mulled Red Cider

ACKNOWLEDGMENTS

Thank you to my all-star team who made this book such a joy. Those who helped "cook this book" include my executive sous-chefs Evan Chender, age 19, whose love of food and commitment to sustainability inspired this book to begin with; Danielle Hartog, age 15; my daughter, Shayna DePersia, age 13; Robyn Kimmel, age 9; and Ian Kimmel, age 16 (founder of kidscook4acause.com). They all loved the kitchen experience—being part of the discovery, creativity, and mastery of cooking with the best ingredients and spinning them into bold new dishes.

The team also included many new friends—you will see their photos and their comments throughout the book. They are: Rose Emily Nelson, age 16; Danny Panton, age 15; Stephanie Maria Lechich, age 17; Sofia Feldmann, age 13; Daniel Glass, age 15; Sophie Hirsch, age 15; Silvan Carlson-Goodman, age 17; Sam Fairey, age 13; Hana Joy Ain, age 13; Peter Hottum, age 15; Steve Burchfield, age 15; Killian Mansfield, age 15; Tom Burchfield, age 15; Philip Chiappone, age 13; Astrid Delgado, age 15; Greg Delgado, age 15; Lauren Slezak, age 15; Brandon Heard, age 13; and Lucia Legnini, age 10.

An enormous hug to the parents behind the scene: Helen Kimmel, MS, RD, who has guided me with her formidable expertise in nutrition for the last ten years; Cindy Hartog; Dr. Judy Nelson; Lili Feldman; and Amy Chender. Also to my dear and brilliant editor, Victoria Wells Arms, and art director, Donna Mark, at Bloomsbury.

To chef Rosalinda Paez, who helped jump-start the project; to Gayle Salomon, who helped test recipes; and to Phil Mansfield, my perspicacious photographer, who captured the spirit of both the cooks and the food with originality and artistry. To my dearest friends whom I hold in my heart; you know who you are. To my beloved husband, Michael Whiteman, who nourishes my life with love and intelligence. —*R. G.*

Thanks to Rozanne for bringing me in on this great project, and thanks to whoever invented the five-second rule. —*P. M.*

INDEX

A

Apple(s)
Apple-Cranberry Sauce, 117
Cinnamon-Apple Muffins, 22
Danielle's Fresh Apple Crisp, 123
Eggless Caesar with Toasted Pecans, Green Apple "Croutons," 78
Oats with Green Apples, Dried Cherries, and Sunflower Seeds, 24
Apple cider
Mulled Red Cider, 149
Onion Soup with Apple Cider and Thyme, 42
Apple cider vinegar
Real French Dressing, 76
Asparagus
Roasted Asparagus with Lemon Drops, 110
Sizzling Skirt Steaks and Lime with Basil, Asparagus, and Cherry Tomatoes, 104
Avocado(s)
Asian Summer Rolls, 64
Avocado Mayonnaise, 56
Great Fish Tacos, 58
Guacamole with Jicama Pick-up Sticks, 72

B

Balsamic vinegar
Balsamic-Rosemary Vinaigrette, 76
Banana(s)
Pineapple-Coconut Frullato, 33
Shayna's Healthy Birthday Cake, 136–137
Very Moist Zucchini-Banana Cake, 138
Barbecue sauce
BBQ Onion and Smoked Gouda Quesadilla, 60
Basil
Pasta Primavera with Jade Zucchini Sauce, 48
Pesto Presto, 38
Sizzling Skirt Steaks and Lime with Basil, Asparagus, and Cherry Tomatoes, 104
"Straw-and-Hay" with Uncooked Tomato Sauce, 46
Summer Tomato Sauce, 45
Bean(s). See also String beans
Chocolate Chili with Cauliflower Popcorn, 92
Beef. See Meat
Bell pepper(s)
Asian Summer Rolls, 64

Juicy Chicken with Roasted Spaghetti Squash, 98
Juicy Red Gazpacho, 36
Mac-and-Cheese with Cauliflower and Creamy Red Pepper Sauce, 52
Pita Fajita, 66
Spicy Thai Tofu with Cashews, Baby Spinach, and Red Peppers, 93
"Tunkalee" with Scrambled Eggs, 23
Black peppercorns, 13
Blueberry(ies)
Blueberry Muffins, 22
Breakfast Crepes with Fresh Blueberry Syrup, 27
Bread
Farmers' Market Pizza, 69
A Loaf of Whole-Wheat Bread, 19
Warm Lemon-Cumin Chicken on Pita Bread Salad, 83
Breadsticks
Prosciutto "Chopsticks," 78
Breakfast, 17
Breakfast Crepes with Fresh Blueberry Syrup, 27
Grape-and-Pignoli Breakfast Cake, 28
Broccoli
Lemony Whole-Wheat Ziti with Broccoli, Parsnips, and Prosciutto, 50
Steamed Broccoli with Cauliflower-Cheddar Sauce, 109
Broth
"Compost" Vegetable Broth, 37
Corncob Broth, 36
Brussels sprouts
Roasted Root Vegetables with Maple Crumbs, 111
Bulgur wheat
Overnight Vegetable Tabbouleh, 86
Burger(s)
Bombay Sliders with Hurry-Curry Sauce, 61
Chickpea Burgers with Fresh Mango Salsa, 62
Butter, 21
Buttermilk
Buttermilk Ice Cream, 142

C

Cabbage
Crunchy Wasabi-Lime Salmon with Red Cabbage and Sugar Snaps, 94
Sloppy Slaw with Carrot-Ginger Dressing, 88
Cake(s)
Chocolate Mousse Cake with Raspberries, 132
Grape-and-Pignoli Breakfast Cake, 28

Hot-Milk Shortcakes with Strawberries and "Cream," 131
Rosemary-Lemon Custard Cakes, 135
Shayna's Healthy Birthday Cake, 136–137
Very Moist Zucchini-Banana Cake, 138
Cantaloupe(s)
Cantaloupe Sherbet, 148
Freshest Fruit Salad with Cinnamon-Sugar Wontons, 128
Irene's Agua Fresca, 147
Carrot(s)
Carrot Curls, 57
Carrot-Ginger-Tomato Soup, 40
Fried Carrot Tops, 40
Ginger-Scallion Brown Rice with Carrot Nibs, 119
Raw Carrot "Fries," 57
Roasted Root Vegetables with Maple Crumbs, 111
Sloppy Slaw with Carrot-Ginger Dressing, 88
Sun-Dried Tomato and Carrot Meatloaf, 103
Sweet Carrot Jam, 21
Cauliflower
Chocolate Chili with Cauliflower Popcorn, 92
"Looks Like Mashed Potatoes," 113
Mac-and-Cheese with Cauliflower and Creamy Red Pepper Sauce, 52
Steamed Broccoli with Cauliflower-Cheddar Sauce, 109
Cheese
BBQ Onion and Smoked Gouda Quesadilla, 60
Bow Ties with Wilted Tomatoes, Spinach, and Feta, 49
Farmers' Market Pizza, 69
Lemon-Parmesan Vinaigrette, 76
"Looks Like Mashed Potatoes," 113
Mac-and-Cheese with Cauliflower and Creamy Red Pepper Sauce, 52
A New Kind of Chicken "Parm" with Roasted Grape Tomatoes, 96
Pesto Presto, 38
Steamed Broccoli with Cauliflower-Cheddar Sauce, 109
Cherry(ies)
Fresh and Spicy Cherry Ices, 145
Oats with Green Apples, Dried Cherries, and Sunflower Seeds, 24
Chicken. See Poultry
Chocolate
Chocolate Chili with Cauliflower Popcorn, 92
Chocolate Mousse Cake with Raspberries, 132

Olive Oil–Chocolate Chip Cookies, 140–141
Shayna's Healthy Birthday Cake, 136–137
Coconut milk
Pineapple-Coconut Frullato, 33
Condiments
Avocado Mayonnaise, 56
Fresh Mango Salsa, 62
Fresh Tomato Chutney, 87
Homemade Butter, 21
Hurry-Curry Sauce, 61
Sriracha Ketchup, 63
Sweet Carrot Jam, 21
Cookies
Olive Oil–Chocolate Chip Cookies, 140–141
Corn
Corncob Broth, 36
Risi e Bisi, 43
Cranberry(ies)
Apple-Cranberry Sauce, 117
Endive Salad with Fancy Greens, Walnuts and Cranberries, Maple Vinaigrette, and Turkey "Pasta," 80
Cucumber(s)
Asian Summer Rolls, 64
Cool Cukes, 57

D

Desserts, 121
Buttermilk Ice Cream, 142
Cantaloupe Sherbet, 148
Chocolate Mousse Cake with Raspberries, 132
Cinnamon-Sugar Wontons, 129
Danielle's Fresh Apple Crisp, 123
Fresh and Spicy Cherry Ices, 145
Freshest Fruit Salad, 128
Honeydew-Kiwi Sorbet, 144
Hot-Milk Shortcakes with Strawberries and "Cream," 131
Maple Snow, 149
Olive Oil–Chocolate Chip Cookies, 140–141
Roasted Pears with Toasted Almonds, Maple Drizzle, 127
Rosemary-Lemon Custard Cakes, 135
Shayna's Healthy Birthday Cake, 136–137
Tower of Peaches, 125
Very Moist Zucchini-Banana Cake, 138
Dinners, 91
Chocolate Chili with Cauliflower Popcorn, 92
Crunchy Wasabi-Lime Salmon with Red Cabbage and Sugar Snaps, 94
Juicy Chicken with Roasted Spaghetti Squash, 98

A New Kind of Chicken
  "Parm" with Roasted Grape
  Tomatoes, 96
Orange-Molasses Sticky Pork
  with Blasted String Beans, 100
Sizzling Skirt Steaks and Lime
  with Basil, Asparagus, and
  Cherry Tomatoes, 104
Spicy Thai Tofu with Cashews,
  Baby Spinach, and Red
  Peppers, 93
Sun-Dried Tomato and Carrot
  Meatloaf, 103
Drinks, 121
  Fresh Strawberry Breeze, 148
  Hot Strawberry Tea, 151
  Iced Green-Lemongrass Tea, 150
  Irene's Agua Fresca, 147
  Mulled Red Cider, 149
  Pineapple-Coconut Frullato, 33
  "Pink Flamingo" Yogurt
    Smoothie, 30
  Watermelon Lemonade, 146

E

Egg(s)
  boiling, 85
  buying, 12
  Rosemary-Lemon Custard
    Cakes, 135
  Tuna-Pasta Niçoise with Sweet
    Peas, 85
  "Tunkalee" with Scrambled
    Eggs, 23
Equipment, 14

F

Fish, 12
  Crunchy Wasabi-Lime Salmon
    with Red Cabbage and Sugar
    Snaps, 94
  Great Fish Tacos, 58
  Tuna-Pasta Niçoise with Sweet
    Peas, 85

G

Garnishes, 57
Ginger
  Carrot-Ginger-Tomato Soup, 40
  Ginger-Scallion Brown Rice
    with Carrot Nibs, 119
  Orange-Ginger Sweet Potato
    Puree, 115
  Sloppy Slaw with Carrot-
    Ginger Dressing, 88
Granola
  Danielle's Fresh Apple Crisp, 123
Grape(s)
  Grape-and-Pignoli Breakfast
    Cake, 28
  Grape Clusters, 57

Greek yogurt
  Breakfast Crepes with Fresh
    Blueberry Syrup, 27
  Hot-Milk Shortcakes with
    Strawberries and "Cream," 131
  Roasted Pears with Toasted
    Almonds, Maple Drizzle, 127

H

Herb(s), 57. See also Basil;
    Rosemary; Thyme
  Fresh Herb Vinaigrette, 76
  Hot and Crusty Stuffed
    Tomatoes, 112
  Juicy Chicken with Roasted
    Spaghetti Squash, 98
  Tower of Peaches, 125
Honeydew
  Honeydew-Kiwi Sorbet, 144
  Irene's Agua Fresca, 147
Hot peppers. See Pepper(s), hot
Hot sauce
  Juicy Red Gazpacho, 36
  Sizzling Skirt Steaks and Lime
    with Basil, Asparagus, and
    Cherry Tomatoes, 104
  Spicy Sesame Noodles with
    Crunchy Snow Peas, 51
  Sriracha Ketchup, 63

I

Ice cream and ices
  Buttermilk Ice Cream, 142
  Cantaloupe Sherbet, 148
  Fresh and Spicy Cherry Ices, 145
  Honeydew-Kiwi Sorbet, 144
  Maple Snow, 149

J

Jalapeño pepper(s)
  Guacamole with Jicama
    Pick-up Sticks, 72
Jam
  Sweet Carrot Jam, 21
Jicama
  Guacamole with Jicama
    Pick-up Sticks, 72

K

Kiwi(s)
  Freshest Fruit Salad with
    Cinnamon-Sugar Wontons, 128
  Honeydew-Kiwi Sorbet, 144

L

Lemon(s)
  Buttermilk Ice Cream, 142
  Fresh and Spicy Cherry Ices, 145
  Hot Strawberry Tea, 151

Lemon-Parmesan Vinaigrette, 76
Lemony Whole-Wheat Ziti
  with Broccoli, Parsnips, and
  Prosciutto, 50
Maple Snow, 149
Roasted Asparagus with Lemon
  Drops, 110
Rosemary-Lemon Custard
  Cakes, 78, 135
Sweet Carrot Jam, 21
Warm Lemon-Cumin Chicken
  on Pita Bread Salad, 83
Watermelon Lemonade, 146
Whole-Wheat Couscous with
  Sweet Peas and Lemon, 118
Winter Tomato Sauce, 45
Lemongrass
  Iced Green-Lemongrass Tea, 150
Lettuce
  Asian Summer Rolls, 64
  Eggless Caesar with Toasted
    Pecans, Green Apple
    "Croutons," 78
  Endive Salad with Fancy
    Greens, Walnuts and
    Cranberries, Maple
    Vinaigrette, and Turkey
    "Pasta," 80
Lime(s)
  Avocado Mayonnaise, 56
  Crunchy Wasabi-Lime Salmon
    with Red Cabbage and Sugar
    Snaps, 94
  Guacamole with Jicama
    Pick-up Sticks, 72
  Honeydew-Kiwi Sorbet, 144
  Iced Green-Lemongrass Tea, 150
  Pita Fajita, 66
  Sizzling Skirt Steaks and Lime
    with Basil, Asparagus, and
    Cherry Tomatoes, 104

M

Mango(es), 30
  Asian Summer Rolls, 64
  Chickpea Burgers with Fresh
    Mango Salsa, 62
  "Pink Flamingo" Yogurt
    Smoothie, 30
Maple syrup
  Danielle's Fresh Apple Crisp, 123
  Maple Snow, 149
  Maple Vinaigrette, 80
  Roasted Pears with Toasted
    Almonds, Maple Drizzle, 127
  Roasted Root Vegetables with
    Maple Crumbs, 111
Mayonnaise
  Avocado Mayonnaise, 56
Meat, 12
  Lemony Whole-Wheat Ziti
    with Broccoli, Parsnips, and
    Prosciutto, 50

Orange-Molasses Sticky Pork
  with Blasted String Beans, 100
Pita Fajita, 66
Prosciutto "Chopsticks," 78
Sizzling Skirt Steaks and Lime
  with Basil, Asparagus, and
  Cherry Tomatoes, 104
Sun-Dried Tomato and Carrot
  Meatloaf, 103
Menus, 152–155
Milk, 12. See also Buttermilk
  Hot-Milk Shortcakes with
    Strawberries and "Cream," 131
Molasses
  Orange-Molasses Sticky Pork
    with Blasted String Beans, 100
Muffin(s)
  Blueberry Muffins, 22
  Cinnamon-Apple Muffins, 22
  Country Pear Muffins, 22

N

Nuts and seeds
  Eggless Caesar with Toasted
    Pecans, Green Apple
    "Croutons," 78
  Endive Salad with Fancy
    Greens, Walnuts and
    Cranberries, Maple
    Vinaigrette, and Turkey
    "Pasta," 80
  Grape-and-Pignoli Breakfast
    Cake, 28
  Hot and Crusty Stuffed
    Tomatoes, 112
  Oats with Green Apples, Dried
    Cherries, and Sunflower
    Seeds, 24
  Overnight Vegetable
    Tabbouleh, 86
  Peanut Butter Hummus with
    Crudités, 73
  Pesto Presto, 38
  Pita Fajita, 66
  Roasted Pears with Toasted
    Almonds, Maple Drizzle, 127
  Spicy Thai Tofu with Cashews,
    Baby Spinach, and Red
    Peppers, 93
  Toasting Nuts, 78

O

Oats
  Oats with Green Apples, Dried
    Cherries, and Sunflower
    Seeds, 24
Onion(s). See also Scallions
  BBQ Onion and Smoked
    Gouda Quesadilla, 60
  Onion Soup with Apple Cider
    and Thyme, 42
  Pink Pickled Onions, 77

Pita Fajita, 66
Silver-Dollar Potato Pancakes, 116
"Tunkalee" with Scrambled
   Eggs, 23
Very Fresh Vegetable Soup, 38
Orange(s)
Bow Ties with Wilted Tomatoes,
   Spinach, and Feta, 49
Chocolate Mousse Cake with
   Raspberries, 132
Mulled Red Cider, 149
Orange-Ginger Sweet Potato
   Puree, 115
Orange juice
Danielle's Fresh Apple Crisp,
   123
Orange-Molasses Sticky Pork
   with Blasted String Beans, 100
Pineapple-Coconut Frullato, 33
Sloppy Slaw with Carrot-
   Ginger Dressing, 88
Organic food, 12

P

Panko
Chickpea Burgers with Fresh
   Mango Salsa, 62
Hot and Crusty Stuffed
   Tomatoes, 112
Roasted Root Vegetables with
   Maple Crumbs, 111
Pantry staples, 13
Parsnip(s)
Lemony Whole-Wheat Ziti
   with Broccoli, Parsnips, and
   Prosciutto, 50
Roasted Root Vegetables with
   Maple Crumbs, 111
Very Fresh Vegetable Soup, 38
Pasta, 44
Bow Ties with Wilted Tomatoes,
   Spinach, and Feta, 49
Lemony Whole-Wheat Ziti
   with Broccoli, Parsnips, and
   Prosciutto, 50
Mac-and-Cheese with
   Cauliflower and Creamy
   Red Pepper Sauce, 52
Pasta Primavera with Jade
   Zucchini Sauce, 48
Spicy Sesame Noodles with
   Crunchy Snow Peas, 51
"Straw-and-Hay" with
   Uncooked Tomato Sauce, 46
Tuna-Pasta Niçoise with Sweet
   Peas, 85
Whole-Wheat Couscous with
   Sweet Peas and Lemon, 118
Pea(s)
Crunchy Wasabi-Lime Salmon
   with Red Cabbage and Sugar
   Snaps, 94
Risi e Bisi, 43

Spicy Sesame Noodles with
   Crunchy Snow Peas, 51
Tuna-Pasta Niçoise with Sweet
   Peas, 85
Whole-Wheat Couscous with
   Sweet Peas and Lemon, 118
Peach(es)
Chickpea Burgers with Fresh
   Mango Salsa, 62
Tower of Peaches, 125
Peanut butter
Peanut Butter Hummus with
   Crudités, 73
Spicy Sesame Noodles with
   Crunchy Snow Peas, 51
Pear(s)
Country Pear Muffins, 22
Roasted Pears with Toasted
   Almonds, Maple Drizzle, 127
Pepper(s), hot
Guacamole with Jicama
   Pick-up Sticks, 72
String Bean Salad with Fresh
   Tomato Chutney, 87
Pepper(s), sweet. See Bell
   pepper(s)
Pineapple(s), 129
Freshest Fruit Salad with
   Cinnamon-Sugar Wontons, 128
Pineapple-Coconut Frullato, 33
Pizza
Farmers' Market Pizza, 69
Pork. See Meat
Potato(es)
"Looks Like Mashed Potatoes,"
   113
Silver-Dollar Potato Pancakes, 116
Poultry, 12
Bombay Sliders with Hurry-
   Curry Sauce, 61
Endive Salad with Fancy
   Greens, Walnuts and
   Cranberries, Maple
   Vinaigrette, and Turkey
   "Pasta," 80
Juicy Chicken with Roasted
   Spaghetti Squash, 98
A New Kind of Chicken
   "Parm" with Roasted Grape
   Tomatoes, 96
Warm Lemon-Cumin Chicken
   on Pita Bread Salad, 83
Processed foods, 11
Prosciutto. See Meat

R

Raspberry(ies)
Breakfast Crepes with Fresh
   Blueberry Syrup, 27
Chocolate Mousse Cake with
   Raspberries, 132
Rhubarb
Fresh Rhubarb Sauce, 117

Rice
Ginger-Scallion Brown Rice
   with Carrot Nibs, 119
Risi e Bisi, 43
Rice paper
Asian Summer Rolls, 64
Rice vinegar
Fun Sauce, 64
Maple Vinaigrette, 80
Orange-Molasses Sticky Pork
   with Blasted String Beans,
   100
Pink Pickled Onions, 77
Sloppy Slaw with Carrot-
   Ginger Dressing, 88
Spicy Sesame Noodles with
   Crunchy Snow Peas, 51
Ripeness, 10
Roasting vegetables, 108
Rosemary
Balsamic-Rosemary
   Vinaigrette, 76
Pink Pickled Onions, 77
Rosemary-Lemon Custard
   Cakes, 135

S

Safety, 15
Salad(s), 71
Create-Your-Own Seasonal
   "House" Salad, 74–75
Eggless Caesar with Toasted
   Pecans, Green Apple
   "Croutons," 78
Endive Salad with Fancy
   Greens, Walnuts and
   Cranberries, Maple
   Vinaigrette, and Turkey
   "Pasta," 80
Freshest Fruit Salad with
   Cinnamon-Sugar Wontons, 128
Guacamole with Jicama
   Pick-up Sticks, 72
Overnight Vegetable
   Tabbouleh, 86
Peanut Butter Hummus with
   Crudités, 73
Sloppy Slaw with Carrot-
   Ginger Dressing, 88
String Bean Salad with Fresh
   Tomato Chutney, 87
Tuna-Pasta Niçoise with Sweet
   Peas, 85
Warm Lemon-Cumin Chicken
   on Pita Bread Salad, 83
Salad dressing(s)
Balsamic-Rosemary
   Vinaigrette, 76
Caesar, 78
Carrot-Ginger Dressing, 88
Fresh Herb Vinaigrette, 76
Lemon-Parmesan Vinaigrette, 76
Maple Vinaigrette, 80

Niçoise Dressing, 85
Real French Dressing, 76
Salt, 13
Saturated fats, 11
Sauce(s)
Apple-Cranberry Sauce, 117
Cauliflower-Cheddar Sauce, 109
Fresh Blueberry Syrup, 27
Fresh Rhubarb Sauce, 117
Fresh Strawberry Sauce, 148
Fun Sauce, 64
Jade Zucchini Sauce, 48
Pesto Presto, 38
Summer Tomato Sauce, 45
Uncooked Tomato Sauce, 46
Winter Tomato Sauce, 45
Scallion(s)
Fun Sauce, 64
Ginger-Scallion Brown Rice
   with Carrot Nibs, 119
Seeds. See Nuts and seeds
Sesame oil
Fun Sauce, 64
Spicy Sesame Noodles with
   Crunchy Snow Peas, 51
Sherry vinegar
Juicy Red Gazpacho, 36
Side dishes, 107
Fabulous Creamed Spinach, 114
Ginger-Scallion Brown Rice
   with Carrot Nibs, 119
Hot and Crusty Stuffed
   Tomatoes, 112
"Looks Like Mashed Potatoes,"
   113
Orange-Ginger Sweet Potato
   Puree, 115
Roasted Asparagus with Lemon
   Drops, 110
Roasted Root Vegetables with
   Maple Crumbs, 111
Silver-Dollar Potato Pancakes, 116
Steamed Broccoli with
   Cauliflower-Cheddar Sauce, 109
Whole-Wheat Couscous with
   Sweet Peas and Lemon, 118
Snow peas
Spicy Sesame Noodles with
   Crunchy Snow Peas, 51
Soup
Carrot-Ginger-Tomato Soup, 40
"Compost" Vegetable Broth, 37
Corncob Broth, 36
Juicy Red Gazpacho, 36
Onion Soup with Apple Cider
   and Thyme, 42
Very Fresh Vegetable Soup, 38
Soy sauce
Fun Sauce, 64
Spicy Sesame Noodles with
   Crunchy Snow Peas, 51
Spicy Thai Tofu with Cashews,
   Baby Spinach, and Red
   Peppers, 93

Spinach
  Bow Ties with Wilted Tomatoes,
    Spinach, and Feta, 49
  Fabulous Creamed Spinach, 114
  Spicy Thai Tofu with Cashews,
    Baby Spinach, and Red
    Peppers, 93
  Very Fresh Vegetable Soup, 38
Squash (summer)
  Farmers' Market Pizza, 69
Squash (winter)
  Juicy Chicken with Roasted
    Spaghetti Squash, 98
  Very Fresh Vegetable Soup, 38
Sriracha. *See* Hot sauce
Steak. *See* Meat
Steaming vegetables, 108
Strawberry(ies)
  Freshest Fruit Salad with
    Cinnamon-Sugar
    Wontons, 128
  Fresh Strawberry Breeze, 148
  Fresh Strawberry Sauce, 148
  Hot-Milk Shortcakes with
    Strawberries and "Cream," 131
  Hot Strawberry Tea, 151
  Maple Snow, 149
  "Pink Flamingo" Yogurt
    Smoothie, 30
  Shayna's Healthy Birthday
    Cake, 136–137
String beans
  Orange-Molasses Sticky Pork
    with Blasted String Beans, 100
  String Bean Salad with Fresh
    Tomato Chutney, 87
  Tuna-Pasta Niçoise with Sweet
    Peas, 85
Sun-dried tomato(es)
  Sun-Dried Tomato and Carrot
    Meatloaf, 103
Sweet potato(es)
  Orange-Ginger Sweet Potato
    Puree, 115

T

Tabbouleh
  Overnight Vegetable
    Tabbouleh, 86
Tahini
  Pita Fajita, 66
Tea
  Hot Strawberry Tea, 151
  Iced Green-Lemongrass Tea, 150
  Mulled Red Cider, 149
Thyme
  Lemon-Parmesan Vinaigrette, 76
  Onion Soup with Apple Cider
    and Thyme, 42
Tofu
  Spicy Thai Tofu with Cashews,
    Baby Spinach, and Red
    Peppers, 93

Tomato(es)
  BBQ Onion and Smoked
    Gouda Quesadilla, 60
  Bombay Sliders with Hurry-
    Curry Sauce, 61
  Bow Ties with Wilted Tomatoes,
    Spinach, and Feta, 49
  Carrot-Ginger-Tomato Soup, 40
  Chocolate Chili with
    Cauliflower Popcorn, 92
  Farmers' Market Pizza, 69
  Grape Tomato Skewers, 57
  Great Fish Tacos, 58
  Guacamole with Jicama
    Pick-up Sticks, 72
  Hot and Crusty Stuffed
    Tomatoes, 112
  Juicy Chicken with Roasted
    Spaghetti Squash, 98
  Juicy Red Gazpacho, 36
  A New Kind of Chicken
    "Parm" with Roasted Grape
    Tomatoes, 96
  Overnight Vegetable
    Tabbouleh, 86
  Pita Fajita, 66
  Sizzling Skirt Steaks and Lime
    with Basil, Asparagus, and
    Cherry Tomatoes, 104
  "Straw-and-Hay" with
    Uncooked Tomato Sauce, 46
  String Bean Salad with Fresh
    Tomato Chutney, 87
  Summer Tomato Sauce, 45
  Sun-Dried Tomato and Carrot
    Meatloaf, 103
  Tuna-Pasta Niçoise with Sweet
    Peas, 85
  "Tunkalee" with Scrambled
    Eggs, 23
  Very Fresh Vegetable Soup, 38
  Warm Lemon-Cumin Chicken
    on Pita Bread Salad, 83
  Winter Tomato Sauce, 45
Tortilla(s)
  BBQ Onion and Smoked
    Gouda Quesadilla, 60
  Great Fish Tacos, 58
Turkey. *See* Poultry
Turnip(s)
  Roasted Root Vegetables with
    Maple Crumbs, 111

V

Vinegar
  Balsamic-Rosemary
    Vinaigrette, 76
  Fresh Herb Vinaigrette, 76
  Fun Sauce, 64
  Juicy Red Gazpacho, 36
  Maple Vinaigrette, 80
  Orange-Molasses Sticky Pork
    with Blasted String Beans, 100

  Pink Pickled Onions, 77
  Real French Dressing, 76
  Sloppy Slaw with Carrot-
    Ginger Dressing, 88
  Spicy Sesame Noodles with
    Crunchy Snow Peas, 51

W

Wasabi peas
  Crunchy Wasabi-Lime Salmon
    with Red Cabbage and Sugar
    Snaps, 94
Watermelon
  Watermelon Lemonade, 146
White wine vinegar
  Fresh Herb Vinaigrette, 76
Wonton wrappers
  Cinnamon-Sugar Wontons, 129
  Tower of Peaches, 125

Y

Yogurt. *See also* Greek Yogurt
  "Pink Flamingo" Yogurt
    Smoothie, 30

Z

Zucchini
  Chickpea Burgers with Fresh
    Mango Salsa, 62
  Farmers' Market Pizza, 69
  Overnight Vegetable
    Tabbouleh, 86
  Pasta Primavera with Jade
    Zucchini Sauce, 48
  Very Fresh Vegetable Soup, 38
  Very Moist Zucchini-Banana
    Cake, 138

GET COOKING!

"They taste better than fries when they get all nice and crispy!"

· · · · · · · · · ·

SHAYNA

"Some people like to draw or paint, but for me, cooking is one of the ways I love to express myself. I like to show people I care about them by cooking their favorite foods and watching their faces when they eat."

· · · · · · · · · ·

ROBYN

MAGICAL

EXCITING FLAVORS

"I like to feed my family what I cook."

· · · · · · · · · ·

DAN

"Seeing how easy it is to make something fancy like crepes made me realize that I can cook anything I want."

· · · · · · · · · ·

IAN

"It was so incredibly easy, but then it came out of the oven and looked like it could be served at a five-star restaurant. It was gorgeous!"

· · · · · · · · · ·

DANIELLE

SUPER DRINK

BEAUTIFUL AND DELICIOUS

A YUMMY SAUCE

"I like to think of new ways to use the flavors and ingredients I like best. I love to go to the farmers' market and buy some fruit and vegetables that are new to me, then go home and taste each one."

· · · · · · · · · ·

ROBYN

AMAZING FLAVOR

"Cooking is like doing a lab experiment, only you get to eat the results!"

· · · · · · · · · ·

IAN

"The soup was so satisfying, but also very light. You could just feel all the vitamins rushing into you!"

· · · · · · · · · ·

DANIELLE

TASTY

"I loved the Rosemary Custard Cakes so much! There was an extra one and we all fought over it. I will make this all the time. They are amazingly great!"

· · · · · · · · · ·

SOPHIE

OVER-NIGHT SENSATION

"I never thought it possible that kids like us could make food like this!"

· · · · · · · · · ·

STEPH

"I always make things spicy, to see how hot I can take it."

· · · · · · · · · ·

DAN

"I never thought I could make ice cream better than store-bought!"

· · · · · · · · · ·

STEPH